D

MAN BITES DOG

It's become a standard piece of advice to aspiring journalists that if a dog bites a man there's no story, but if a man bites a dog — well, that's *news*. The saying 'man bites dog' can be traced back to a poem by Oliver Goldsmith entitled 'Elegy on the Death of a Mad Dog'. It tells the story of a dog that went mad and bit a man and ends with the lines:

The man recover'd of the bite,
The dog it was that died.

The poem passed into popular folklore and a number of new versions appeared, including, it's believed, a funny one in which a man *did* bite a dog — hence the advice of editors to their journalists.

About the Author

June Whitfield became a household name with the radio series 'Take It From Here' when she played Eth, the long-suffering fiancée. She still enjoys radio work and can be heard regularly on Radio 2 in *The News Huddlines* with Roy Hudd.

She has co-starred on television with many of our most famous comedians, but is best known for the series 'Terry and June' with Terry Scott.

June Whitfield lives in Wimbledon with her husband, Tim Aitchison and Rabbit, her Tibetan terrier/Jack Russell cross breed. They have one daughter, Suzy, who is also an actress.

Dogs' Tales

June Whitfield

NEW ENGLISH LIBRARY
Hodder and Stoughton

Copyright © 1987 by June Whitfield

First published in Great Britain in 1987 by Robson Books Ltd

First New English Library paperback edition 1988

Cartoons by John Donegan
Designed by Harold King

British Library C.I.P.

Whitfield, June
Dogs' tales.
1. Pets : Dogs – Stories, anecdotes
I. Title
636.7

ISBN 0 450 48907 8

Printed and bound in Great Britain for Hodder and Stoughton paperbacks, a division of Hodder and Stoughton Ltd., Mill Road, Dunton Green, Sevenoaks, Kent TN13 2YA (Editorial Office: 47 Bedford Square, London WC1B 3DP) by Cox & Wyman Ltd., Reading.

In fond memory of
'Sid' 1964–79

CONTENTS

ACKNOWLEDGEMENTS

Thanks to all the following for their assistance in supplying information, and particularly to all those charities who do such impressive work on behalf of dogs and their owners.

The Guide Dogs for the Blind Association, The National Canine Defence League, The Kennel Club, RSPCA, PRO DOGS, Search and Rescue Dogs Association, St Andrew Animal Fund, The Metropolitan Police, Hearing Dogs for the Deaf, The Dogs Home Battersea, The National Anti-Vivisection Society, HM Customs and Excise, Spillers Foods, Pedigree Petfoods, Harrods, Get Stuffed.

INTRODUCTION

I'd better start this introduction by coming clean and admitting that I haven't been a dog-lover all my life. I grew up in a household where we had (sorry about this) *cats*. Then I met my husband, Tim, who introduced me to Sid – and that was it. I've barely been able to look a cat in the eye since then in case it senses my betrayal.

Sid was our first puppy, a Golden Labrador who was absolutely typical of his breed – intelligent and good-tempered, a dog who gave us tremendous pleasure and very few problems. His great obsession in life was swimming which, as anyone who's ever had to load a soaking dog into the back seat of the car or live with the smell of damp fur will know, has its problems. On his daily walks on Wimbledon Common, near where we live, he had to be hurried past the pond before being let off the lead. Usually he behaved himself but occasionally the temptation would be too much and he'd turn tail, race back and jump in. When he got home, still soaked, he'd try to look repentant, and although we knew he wasn't sincere we couldn't hold it against him.

He was always very playful and loved burying and digging up things, a habit which one spring led to a minor disaster. At that time we had a tortoise but after a very long and cold winter it sadly didn't emerge from hibernation. Our daughter Suzy, who's now an actress, was devastated and so we decided to give the poor thing a proper burial in the back garden. It was laid to rest with full ceremony and the funeral party had just made its way solemnly back to the house when Sid caught up with us with something in his mouth. After all our efforts he'd dug up the tortoise and retrieved it for us. Father returned to the spot to dig a deeper hole!

Sid was one of the family and when he died we didn't try to replace him. We'd been without a dog for a couple of years or so when Jimmy Edwards, with whom I'd worked in *Take It From Here* and on TV, asked if we'd mind looking after his dog for a few weeks. Jim's dog was called Rubu, which is Swahili for 'moustache', and he was the kind of cheerful, charming, scruffy cross-breed that gives mongrels a good name. His Tibetan terrier mother, Dill, lives with Biddy Fletcher, a great friend of both Jim and ourselves. Dill had had a fling with the local Jack Russell and Rubu, the result, was a wonderful combination that fooled even the experts. When he met that doyenne of the dog world, Barbara Woodhouse, on a TV programme she confidently told him he was a Norfolk terrier!

We enjoyed having him to stay very much, but for his own sake when Jim asked if we'd look after him for several months while he went to Australia we said we thought it was a bit unsettling for the poor dog to be passed backwards and forwards. And that was how we came to own Rubu.

We didn't intend to change his name, but after a while Tim got fed-up explaining to the other dog-walkers on the Common that he wasn't called Ruby. At the time we also had a pet rabbit called Guti, who was a wonderful paper shredder. If we ever wanted to get rid of any old letters or documents we'd give them to Guti who reduced them to confetti in minutes! Somehow, out of all this, Rubu was transformed into Rabbit, and Rabbit he's been ever since. Not that his new name was without its pitfalls. Tim was walking him on the Common early one morning when they met a man exercising six greyhounds on leashes. 'Rabbit!' he called. The greyhounds pricked up their ears.

'You'd better watch it or they'll have him,' warned their owner.

For such a small dog Rabbit sets his sights high. He loves chasing things; anything will do, from squirrels and cats to Dobermanns. But above all he likes to chase deer. We've lost him on several occasions when we've been out in the country, one time in the pitch dark when we were staying with Frankie Howerd (who, incidentally, is one of Rabbit's greatest admirers). Four of us searched for nearly two hours until finally the culprit emerged from a hedge looking very pleased with himself and with a 'Did somebody call me?' expression on his face. We could only hope that he hadn't been worrying sheep or deer. It's a bad habit, not to say a dangerous one, and we do all we can to limit his opportunities. Once we went away for a weekend to a lovely hotel in Wales and had a terrific time except for the fact that every field in sight was full of sheep. Rabbit sat by the window licking his lips and trying to pretend that he hadn't noticed them. In the end we had to drive eight miles to find the nearest sheep-free zone.

He was also inclined to rush after large dogs and not come back when called. I mentioned this to Katie Boyle when I met her at a lunch one day and she recommended a Mr Fisher who specialises in dog training. Mr Fisher came to see us and took Rabbit out on to the Common; immediately he set off in pursuit of another dog, at which Mr Fisher blew a short blast on a rape whistle and jangled some metal discs. The noise was devastating and stopped Rabbit in his tracks – not to mention some of the passers-by! After a couple more blasts he'd begun to learn his lesson and responded to the jangle of the discs without the noise of the whistle. These days whenever Rabbit goes out for a walk the discs go too, and he's learned to come back whenever he hears them rattling.

I hope I haven't made him sound a difficult dog because he's not, he's a fun dog. He loves travelling in the front seat of the car – usually on my lap – and always looking out, except on motorways when he takes a nap. He's a great character, very alert and interested in what's going on around him; he hates being left behind and always gives us a wonderful welcome when we come home. We couldn't ask for a more faithful friend.

I hope you'll find this book entertaining and informative – and even useful! I've had a lot of fun working on it and we've uncovered some surprising and amusing facts, but it's also made me realise that although we're supposed to be a nation of dog-lovers we still have a long way to go before we can say that we care enough. You may find a few of the statistics among these pages depressing, but I've included them because I think it's important that we remind ourselves that for every dozen or so dogs who live contented lives, like Rabbit, there's one being mistreated by its owner or waiting to be destroyed in an animal shelter because no one wants it. In buying this book you have already helped the RSPCA in its work, because the royalties from sales are going direct to its funds. Thank you.

Happy reading!

JUNE WHITFIELD
1987

As his personal contribution to this book of canine facts and stories Rabbit Whitfield has compiled his own. Here it is!

RABBIT WHITFIELD – MY STORY

Breed:	Tibetan terrier/Jack Russell cross
Date of birth:	October 1979
Place of birth:	Wisborough Green, West Sussex
Mother's name:	Dill
Father's name:	Dudley
Favourite food:	Smoked salmon and cheese (particularly Cheddar)
Dislikes:	Chocolate, yoghurt and sweets (*really!*)
Best friends:	Bryn: black mongrel (mainly Labrador)
	Puppy and Sooty; half-sisters
	Senter; German pointer
Holidays:	I go to the country to stay with my mother and half-sisters or to stay with Bryn
Sleeps:	Officially on a chair in the bedroom, but I usually manage to sneak on to the bed

Favourite things:	A daily walk on Wimbledon Common
	Cleaning my whiskers on the best carpet after a meal
	Chasing anything that moves
	Barking in the garden, specially late at night
	Trying to 'kill' the Hoover when it's on
	A place by the fire
	Leaving my dogchews all over the house for people to trip over
My day to remember:	12 December 1985, when my owner, June, went to Buckingham Palace to receive the OBE, I had to stay at home – I suppose they didn't want me fighting with those corgis – but I celebrated with a special smoked salmon lunch!
Pet hates:	Cats and squirrels: can't catch them
	Anything that drops through the letterbox
	Visits to the vet, specially when needles are involved

RABBIT
1987

DOGS
AND THEIR
PEOPLE

THE MAN WHO PREFERRED DOGS TO PEOPLE

Most dog owners will admit that they prefer the company of their pets to that of many people, but few take this as far as Francis Henry Egerton, eighth Earl of Bridgewater, who preferred dogs to almost any human and believed that nothing but the best was good enough for them. His particular passion was for shoes – he wore a new pair of shoes or boots every day of the year, and he lined the discarded pairs up around his house where they served as a useful calendar – so he arranged for his dogs to be well-shod too. Each had four soft leather boots made specially by the Earl's personal shoemaker.

Most of his time was spent in the company of dogs. He often took his canine pals out with him for a ride in his carriage and each evening they dined together, with eleven chosen dogs seated around the table dressed in their best clothes, always in the height of fashion, and with napkins tied carefully around their necks. Each dog was attended by a servant, but it was expected to behave itself properly and eat from the plate while its master discussed the news of the day with it. Those guests who didn't behave themselves properly were not invited back until their manners had improved.

TEN ROYAL DOG LOVERS

1 **Elizabeth II** The Queen's enthusiasm for corgis is well known. Perhaps not so well known are her 'dorgis', her dachshund/corgi crosses. The first royal corgi was called Dookie; the Queen's favourite was reported to be called Susan.

2 **George V** King George V had a Sealyham called Happy who wrote a book entitled *If I Were King George.*

3 **Princess Alice** Princess Alice once rescued a terrier called Skippy from the Dogs Home Battersea.

4 **Edward VII** A wirehaired fox terrier called Caesar was the favourite pet of King Edward VII. He wore a collar with the inscription 'I belong to the king' in case he ever got lost. At his master's funeral procession in 1910 he walked immediately behind the gun-carriage that bore the coffin.

5 **Queen Victoria** She was perhaps the greatest of the royal dog-lovers. All kinds of dogs were kept in her kennels, from greyhounds and borzois to pugs and Skye terriers. Her favourite was a King Charles spaniel named Dash, which she used to dress in a red jacket and blue trousers. It's said that on the day of her coronation the new queen returned from Westminster Abbey and promptly rolled up her sleeves and gave Dash a bath.

6 **Charles II** He was the first British monarch to enjoy dog racing. In 1670 he staged the 'Hampton Court Olympic' at which, according to observers, dogs were raced against

each other over a paddock divided into lanes with ropes. His interest didn't do much to promote the sport and it failed to become truly popular until the 1920s. He was also the first monarch to go in for small dogs, which until that time had been considered suitable for ladies only. So crazy was he about the spaniels that have been named after him that they overran the royal chambers. 'God save your Majesty, but God damn your dogs,' his exasperated courtiers are said to have told him.

7 Prince Rupert When Prince Rupert was sent to assist Charles I in the Civil War he was accompanied everywhere, even on the battlefield, by his large white poodle called Boy. Not only was Boy the first poodle seen in England, but he was also believed to possess supernatural powers. The Roundheads were convinced that they would need help to destroy Boy and appealed to America for assistance in overcoming him. He wasn't, sadly, the demon they took him for, and was killed at the Battle of Marston Moor in 1644.

8 James I He loved hunting and kept many dogs. One of his favourite hounds, called Jewel, was shot and killed with a crossbow by his wife, Anne of Denmark, in a hunting accident. The king was furious and referred to the incident for years. When the Archbishop of Canterbury killed a gamekeeper in a similar accident the king consoled him with the assurance that the loss of the man was not as great as the loss of Jewel.

9 Elizabeth I Whether Queen Elizabeth I should be included in a list of royal dog lovers is debatable. She enjoyed hunting and her pack of 'singing' pocket beagles were famous for their noise. But she was also very keen on bull and bear baiting, and didn't flinch from the horrific injuries to the baited animals or the dogs.

10 Mary Queen of Scots Mary Queen of Scots took a dog – probably a small spaniel or a French griffon – to her execution. The dog was hidden beneath her petticoats and was only discovered after the axe had fallen. It had to be dragged away from the body, which it refused to leave, and was given to a French princess who had been a friend of the queen.

FIVE WRITERS AND
THEIR DOGS

John Steinbeck, who took his large French poodle Charley on a 10,000 mile tour of the USA in 1960. They travelled in a truck and camped in the back and their adventures are recorded in *Travels with Charley*.

Alexander Pope, whose huge Great Dane Bounce was admired by everyone. His size and courageous nature came in useful when he accompanied his master on walks because Pope's satirical poem *The Dunciad* had made him many enemies and Bounce supplied some necessary protection.

Sir Walter Scott loved his huge mastiff/deerhound cross Maida more than any other dog. Maida was as big as a Shetland pony and killed lots of foxes, but lived in dread of the family cat, called Hinse or Hinsefield, who bossed all the dogs about and scratched them on the nose if they got too forward.

The Brontë sisters each had dogs. Anne's was a spaniel called Flossy and Emily's was a bull mastiff called Keeper that would do anything for her although no one else could control him. When she died he was quite inconsolable.

J.M. Barrie owned a Newfoundland called Luath on whom he based the character of Nana in *Peter Pan*. The first actor to play Nana on the stage was Arthur Lupino, and he went to Barrie's home to study Luath's movements so that he could copy him.

AND ONE WRITER WHO DENIED BEING A DOG-LOVER

James Thurber wrote about dozens of dogs, and with an affection that convinced many people that he was an ardent dog-lover. This he denied with the words, 'I'm not a dog-lover; to me a dog-lover is a dog in love with another dog . . .'

DIAMOND – THE DOG THAT DIDN'T EXIST

For many, many years people have been telling a famous anecdote about Sir Isaac Newton, who in 1693 suffered a mild nervous breakdown while he was studying at Trinity College, Cambridge. It has always been said that the breakdown occurred because Newton's pet dog, Diamond, knocked over a candle in his master's room and started a fire that destroyed Newton's research and records of many years. Newton, the story went, just looked sorrowfully at the terrible mess and said, 'O Diamond, Diamond, thou little knowest the damage thou hast done.'

It's very touching and it proves that Newton was a dog-lover. The only problem is that not a word of it is true and Diamond never existed!

FOUR FAMOUS TALES

Mrs Patrick Campbell, the English actress famous for her high-handed manners and her wit, owned a Pekingese which she tried to take with her everywhere. On one occasion she attempted to smuggle him through Customs and, figuring that she was so famous no one would search her, tucked the Peke inside her cape. It nearly worked, as she told her friends. 'Everything was going splendidly, until my bosom barked.'

Sir Winston Churchill had a poodle called Rufus who was treated very much as one of the family. At mealtimes his dinner was set out for him on a cloth on the dining-room floor and everyone refrained from starting their own meal until Rufus had been served. After dinner one evening the film of *Oliver Twist* was shown and Rufus sat on Churchill's lap to watch. During a scene when Bill Sikes was going to drown his dog Bull's Eye Churchill put his hands over Rufus's eyes and told him, 'Don't look now, my dear. I shall tell you what happens afterwards.'

Hetty Green was one of the richest women in America, and one of the most strange and reclusive, too. Despite being worth more than $100 million when she died in 1916 she had a reputation for incredible meanness, which included her habit of dressing in old clothes and doing everything on the cheap. Her closest friend was her mongrel dog which, like her, was distinctly antisocial and kept biting people.

Most of her visitors were prepared to put up with it in an attempt to keep in Mrs Green's good books, but one finally told her that she ought to get rid of it. Mrs Green flatly refused. 'He loves me,' she said, 'and he doesn't even know how rich I am.'

Ogden Nash, the American writer, was friendly with radio director Tom Carlson, who owned a dog. One day the dog chewed up a copy of one of Nash's books, which he had specially autographed, and Carlson had to search for a replacement copy which he sent to Nash with an apologetic request that he sign it. Back came the book with the message, 'To Tom Carlson or his dog – depending on whose taste it best suits.'

SIX DOGS IN POWER

---

1 **Blanco**. Blanco was a pure white collie given to President Lyndon Johnson by a girl who lived in Illinois. He was beautiful but because of overbreeding was also totally neurotic. During Johnson's spell in the White House Blanco was kept on tranquillisers, which stopped him biting people, and used to come out and shake hands with visitors for the benefit of the press. When Johnson left office Blanco was swiftly found a new home.

2 Blondi. Blondi was the beautiful Alsatian bitch given to Adolf Hitler by Martin Bormann. She travelled with Hitler, who loved to make her jump through a hoop, climb ladders and scale walls. After fighting with Eva Braun's two West Highland terriers Blondi was banished from social gatherings, but she was there to 'sing' on her master's 54th birthday to a delighted audience. When Hitler retreated to the bunker beneath the Reich Chancellery in Berlin in 1945 she went too, and on 28 April her master tested the efficiency of his cyanide capsules on her. They worked.

3 Checkers. Long before Watergate put an end to his political career, Richard Nixon was accused by opponents of accepting money and gifts for his own personal use. So vocal was the campaign against him that it looked as if he would be dropped from the Republican ranks. In an attempt to defend himself Nixon went on TV and made a long speech during which he talked about his humble origins and the way he'd dragged himself up in life through honest hard work. Yes, he confessed with a tear in his eye, he *had* accepted a gift after his nomination, a spaniel puppy which his children called Checkers and which they adored, and no matter what anyone said they were going to keep it . . . The letters of support came pouring in from dog-lovers in all quarters and, thanks to Checkers, Nixon's career was saved.

4 Dizzy. Named after his master's hero Disraeli, Dizzy has appeared on a number of CND marches and election campaigns with duffel-coated ex-Labour Party leader Michael Foot.

5 Lucky. Lucky the sheepdog has often been seen on television dragging Ronald or Nancy Reagan across the White House lawn.

6 Peritas. The favourite dog of Alexander the Great, Peritas accompanied his master during the great march to India. Normally the cities that Alexander founded along the way were called Alexandria, but one was named Peritas in honour of the faithful dog, and a statue of him was erected in the market square.

DOGS ARE GOOD FOR YOU!

Dogs are good for you, and that's official. It's not much of a surprise to anyone who has ever owned a dog, of course. We may complain at having to take our pets out for walks in the rain and snow, but we all know that we're fitter and happier for it, and it's a small price to pay for the loyalty, companionship and warm welcome that every dog has to offer its owner. Now the scientists and experts have confirmed what dog-owners have known all along. Dogs are a good thing!

This was recognised several years ago in an official report titled *Dogs in the United Kingdom*, which was compiled and published by JACOPIS – the Joint Advisory Committee on Pets in Society. It acknowledged that a growing number of people living in urban areas had problems when it came to keeping a pet, yet that it was people in towns who most had the need for pets. 'Nowhere is this more true, with the breakdown of the family unit, than in the case of a solitary old person whose sole constant companion (and often element of security) is a pet animal,' it concluded.

Recent research has backed this up. Reports in 1983 and

1986 found that people who own pets live longer than those who don't and that children who are brought up with pets have better social skills than kids who live in families without pets. Ownership of a pet has also been shown to raise morale and make people more cheerful.

Among bodies who recognise this is the Royal College of Nursing which has recently backed pet visiting schemes. These involve specially registered dogs and owners who make regular visits to local nursing homes and hospitals so that patients can experience some of the benefits of a pet. If you've got a placid, well-behaved pet and you'd like to spread a little happiness, get in touch with PAT at PRO-DOGS (address on page 46).

Owning a dog isn't just good for your psychological health, either. A 1980 report by Katcher and Friedman indicated a significantly higher survival rate among heart attack victims who owned a pet. This had a lot to do with the fact that handling a pet – and particularly a dog – is good for reducing blood pressure. It's not only the owner's blood pressure that goes down when he or she strokes a dog; the dog's goes down too!

TEN PAINTERS WHO LOVED DOGS

1 **Sir Edwin Landseer** Perhaps the greatest dog-lover among painters was Sir Edwin Landseer. Many artists included dogs in the backgrounds of their pictures but Landseer painted their portraits and captured their personalities in a way that no one else did. Included among his models were his own dogs Brutus, Lassie and Myrtle, many of Queen Victoria's favourite pets and the famous dogs of the day, including Sir Walter Scott's beloved deerhound Maida. Most famous of all was Paul Pry, a beautiful black-and-white Newfoundland whose portrait, entitled 'A Distinguished Member of the Humane Society' was dedicated to the Royal Humane Society. Among admirers of the breed, black-and-white Newfoundlands have been known as Landseers since that time.

2 **George Stubbs** Stubbs is most famous for his classic studies of racehorses but he also painted many pictures of dogs, particularly of sporting dogs and hounds.

3 Sir Thomas Gainsborough Another English painter who included many dogs in his portraits. In his picture entitled 'Mrs Robinson' he includes a large white Pomeranian dog, a breed that had been very rare until that time. He was obviously taken with this particular type of dog because he painted them again in 'Pomeranian Bitch and Puppy'.

4 William Hogarth In his self-portrait 'The Painter and his Dog' Hogarth shows himself in a mirror and his pug, called Trump, sitting beside it. It's not the sort of pug we see today and not a very pretty-looking animal. In fact in some ways it looks rather like its master!

5 Veronese Veronese often included dogs in the background of his paintings. On one occasion this got him into trouble. He included dogs in his painting of the Last Supper, which caused an outcry and accusations of irreligiousness. He got himself out of this sticky situation by renaming the picture 'Feast in the House of Levi', by which title it's known today. Veronese was also the first western artist to paint a Saluki.

6 Rubens In the corner of Rubens's 'Raising of the Cross', which can be seen in Antwerp Cathedral, there's a spaniel. Rubens didn't originally intend to include the dog in the work but just as he was finishing it a priest visited his studio and admired his spaniel. 'A dog like that should not die,' he told the artist. 'How am I supposed to prevent that?' asked Rubens. 'Include him in your picture,' said the priest, and that's how the dog achieved immortality.

7 Velazquez Velazquez painted several pictures of what seems to be the same dog, a huge mastiff. His 'Don Antonio el Ingles' shows an English dwarf at the Spanish court holding the lead of a dog that is nearly as tall as himself. The same elements, dwarves and huge dogs, appear in another picture 'Las Meninas'.

8 Titian Titian's very stately portrait of Charles V shows the emperor holding on to the collar of a very large dog of a breed unknown today – possibly one of the ancient boar hounds which died out during the nineteenth century. In his 'Venus', on show at the Uffizi in Florence, he includes a red and white toy spaniel, one of the first visual records of this breed. In 1576 he painted a portrait which included a study of a papillon. When a standard was being drawn up for the breed in 1934 the model used was Titian's picture, which just goes to show how little some dogs have changed over a period of 350 years!

9 Hieronymus Bosch The first picture of a performing dog is shown in Bosch's painting 'The Conjuror'. Standing behind the conjuror, almost hidden, is a small dog wearing a fool's cap and bells on its head – obviously the conjuror's stooge.

10 Van Dyck Perhaps Van Dyck's most famous dogs are his King Charles spaniels which he included in a portrait of Charles I's sons, but he painted many dogs including, unusually, a beautiful silvery grey Weimaraner in a portrait of Prince Rupprecht of Pfalz in 1631. It's an important clue in helping to trace the history of the breed.

SIX REALLY USEFUL DOGS

All dogs are useful. Some of them work for a living as guard dogs or sheep dogs or sled dogs – more about them later. Even Rabbit has his uses; he keeps our garden free of cats, gets the family exercising on Wimbledon Common, guards us from the postman and cheers us up if ever we feel down. He'd have a go at rounding up sheep, too, if we'd give him the chance! Here are six individual dogs who proved, in one way or another, invaluable to their owners . . .

Toby – the canine critic John Steinbeck had just finished the first draft of *Of Mice and Men* when Toby, his setter puppy, chewed half of it to confetti. Steinbeck was forgiving, despite the fact that it took him two months to complete the work for a second time. 'I didn't want to ruin a good dog for a manuscript I'm not sure is good at all. He got only an ordinary spanking', he wrote. When the work got a poor reception in some quarters he came more firmly to the conclusion that Toby had been a good critic. 'I'm not sure Toby didn't know what he was doing when he ate that first draft. I have promoted Toby-dog to be lieutenant-colonel in charge of literature.'

Barry Barry was the most famous of all Swiss mountain rescue dogs. He was born in 1800 and trained at the hospice of the Great St Bernard Pass, which had been founded in 1049 by St Bernard of Menthen to help pilgrims crossing the pass. By the eighteenth century the monks had trained their huge mastiff dogs to sniff for travellers lost in the snow, dig them out and hug them until they were warm. The breed was first known as the *barihund* (bear-dog) and was christened St Bernard at an English dog show in 1862. Barry saved more than forty people during his career, even carrying one child to safety on his back. In 1812 he rescued a young man who thought he was being attacked by some wild shaggy beast and struck out at the dog with a knife. Although his injuries were not major, Barry was retired and died two years later.

Raton – the diet dog Raton was the kind of pet that many ladies would love. He belonged to the seventeenth-century prostitute Ninon de Lenclos, who carried him everywhere with her. Her career was an extraordinarily long one and in her later years she had to keep a careful watch on her figure. Raton proved invaluable for helping her keep to her diet. Every time she picked up something sweet or fattening to eat, he would bark until she put it down again.

Balto In January 1925 the Alaskan town of Nome was hit by an epidemic of diphtheria. The supply of drugs soon ran out, but the weather was so appalling that there was no way in which a plane could take new supplies to the inhabitants. As a last resort, it was decided to send anti-toxin serum the 655 miles overland on a series of dog-sleds. It was a terrible struggle in weather that grew increasingly worse as time passed. The final sixty-mile leg of the journey was made by Gunnar Kasson and his dog team, which was led by a black husky called Balto. By now the weather was so bad that the trail had been blotted out. The temperature was down to -50°F and an 80 mph blizzard was blowing straight at them. Kasson had no idea where he was; he thought that he and the team were totally lost, but Balto managed to scent the way and kept them going across frozen lagoons and deep drifts of new snow. By the time he led the way into Nome Kasson, the other dogs were exhausted and Balto's feet had been cut to shreds by ice splinters, but they had delivered the drugs in time to save many lives. From start to finish the journey was

675 miles, and the twenty dog teams involved took a total of 127 hours to complete it. A statue to Balto's heroism was erected in Central Park, New York, in 1925 and can still be seen.

Dan In 1899 Edward Elgar wrote the 'Enigma Variations', a collection of tunes dedicated to his friends. One of his friends was George Robertson Sinclair, and it was assumed by many that the variation entitled XI (G.R.S.) was based on *his* personality. Then one day Elgar revealed that his inspiration was actually Dan, an English bulldog who belonged to G.R.S. The music represented an incident when Dan fell down a steep bank of the River Wye, paddled upstream to find a spot to land and barked with joy when he got out. 'Set that to music,' George Robertson Sinclair had challenged.

'I did; here it is,' said Elgar.

Buddy Buddy was the world's first Seeing Eye dog – or guide dog, as we know them in this country. She was an Alsatian bitch bred by a wealthy American woman who lived in Switzerland during the 1920s and she was given to a young American called Morris Frank, who became the first guide dog owner.

NINE DOG ORGANISATIONS

These nine organisations are concerned in whole or part with the welfare and training of dogs.

1 The Dogs Home Battersea.
2 The Guide Dogs for the Blind Association.
3 Hearing Dogs for the Deaf.
4 The Kennel Club.
5 The National Anti-Vivisection Society.
6 National Canine Defence League.
7 PRO DOGS.
8 The Royal Society for the Prevention of Cruelty to Animals.
9 Search and Rescue Dog Association.

THE DOGS HOME BATTERSEA

4 Battersea Park Road   London SW8 4AA

The Dogs Home Battersea began in unlikely circumstances in 1860, when Mrs Mary Tealby went to visit her friend Mrs Major in Islington, north London, and found her nursing a stray dog that she had discovered in the road. At that time it was common to see starving dogs roaming the streets, and when Mrs Tealby and Mrs Major began to collect and tend other local strays they soon realised the size of the task they had set themselves. It was obvious that if they were going to make many inroads into the problem at all they would need funds and a property, and later that year they published a prospectus appealing for help. As a result the Home for Lost and Starving Dogs opened in Holloway in October 1860, accepting all stray and unwanted dogs brought to it. The first annual report carried this statement of their aims:

'The Committee would willingly hope and believe that no one who is capable of appreciating the faithful, affectionate, and devoted nature of the dog, can have seen any of the intelligent creatures lost, emaciated and even dying from starvation, without feeling an earnest wish that there were some means established for rescuing them from so dreadful a death, and restoring them to usefulness.'

Ten years later they moved to their current address in Battersea, where there was more space to continue the work. In 1885 Queen Victoria granted The Dogs Home Battersea, as it is correctly called, Royal Patronage. Since its foundation the home has provided shelter for more than two million lost and stray dogs and, in doing so, become famous worldwide.

The 1985 figures for the Home indicate the sheer scale of the work.

Dogs received (from the police and other sources)	20,542
Dogs destroyed	8,721
Dogs sold	8,396
Dogs claimed by owners	2,871

Discounting mongrels – and it's difficult to do that, because 15, 128 were received – the ten most common breeds brought to the Home in 1985 were:

1	Alsatian	1,162
2	Jack Russell-type	577
3	Labrador retriever	334
4	Collie (all types)	297
5	Dobermann	292
6	Greyhound	209
7	Spaniel (all types)	187
8	Yorkshire terrier	145
9	Lurcher	131
10	Bull terrier	103

Nearly every recognised breed of dog turns up at the Home in the course of a year, though the more rare the breed, the smaller the numbers. The least common breeds of 1985, notching up only one admission each, were:

1 Bichon frise
2 Briard
3 Griffon
4 Groenendael
5 Keeshond
6 Kerry Blue
7 Lakeland terrier
8 Manchester terrier
9 Miniature pinscher
10 Newfoundland
11 Pomeranian
12 Pug
13 Rhodesian ridgeback
14 Sealyham
15 Skye terrier
16 Wolfhound

Through the years Battersea has provided loyal companions for many thousands of people who have been prepared to take on stray and unwanted dogs. If you're looking for a pet and you're not worried too much about its pedigree, why not go along for a visit?

THE GUIDE DOGS FOR THE BLIND ASSOCIATION

Alexandra House 9 Park Street Windsor Berks SL4 1JR

During World War I a young German doctor was walking in the hospital grounds with a blind man and his own Alsatian dog when he was called away. The doctor left the dog with the man and was so impressed with the way it behaved with him and its understanding of his problem that he decided to try some experiments to see if guide dogs could be trained to help the blind. The work which he conducted at Potsdam attracted the attention of a wealthy American lady, Mrs Dorothy Eustis, who bred and trained Alsatians in Switzerland for use in the customs service and the police.

After a visit to Potsdam Mrs Eustis was so impressed that she wrote a feature for the American paper the *Saturday Evening Post* in October 1927. Only a few days later a young blind man called Morris Frank heard about the article and bought a copy of the paper for five cents. It was a worthwhile investment. Those five cents 'bought an article that was worth more than a million dollars to me. It changed my whole life,' he said later. He was so excited by the idea of a guide dog that he wrote to Mrs Eustis asking for help and offering his services in the training of the dogs. Before long Morris Frank was on his way to Germany, to become America's first guide dog owner. He and his dog Buddy returned to the USA and did much to establish the training of guide dogs there.

In Britain a trial scheme was set up in 1931 in Wallasey with a trainer lent by Mrs Eustis whose L'Oeil qui Voit (The Seeing Eye) centre in Switzerland was attracting worldwide interest. The first four British guide dogs and owners to be trained were Allen Caldwell and Flash, G.W.Lamb and Meta, Musgrave Frankland and Judy and Thomas Ap Rhys and Folly. All four dogs were Alsatians and their effect on their owners was spectacular. Musgrave Frankland put it quite simply: 'A guide dog is almost equal in many ways to giving a blind man sight itself. Judith has been worth her weight in gold . . . I would not be without her for a day.'

From this small beginning has grown a national charity that today trains about 700 guide dogs a year and has its own breeding stock of around 250 bitches and dogs, chosen specially for their temperament and physical stamina and size. Most guide dogs are now Labradors or golden retriever crosses, with a small number of Alsatians and other dogs such as collies making up the numbers. And each year more than five hundred new owners find their lives revolutionised by these wonderful, hard-working animals.

Five things you should know about guide dogs:

1 In 1985 there were 3,650 guide dogs in Britain.

2 So that there is no financial bar to owning a guide dog, blind students can 'buy' a dog for 50p.

3 It costs £1,000 and takes more than a year to put a guide dog through training.

4 When it is leading its owner a guide dog has to concentrate hard, so never touch it, pat it, feed it or otherwise distract it from what it's doing. Not only will you ruin its concentration but you may endanger the life of its owner.

5 If you are in a vehicle and see a guide dog waiting at the kerb to cross the road, don't stop for it unless it's at a crossing or a light is against you. The dog will be looking for a suitable gap in the traffic and by stopping unexpectedly you will confuse it. You should also avoid hooting your horn or shouting at a dog to signal it to cross a road or doing anything out of the ordinary.

HEARING DOGS FOR THE DEAF

**Training Centre   Little Close   Lower Icknield Way
Lewknor   Oxon OX9 5RY**

What guide dogs do for people who are blind, hearing dogs do for the deaf. After successful experiments in the USA the Hearing Dogs for the Deaf charity began its work in Britain in 1982 and to date 300 dogs have been trained to provide 'ears' for their owners. No one breed is better than another at the work, but hearing dogs are selected for their personalities and trained individually to meet the needs of each owner. All the trained dogs are capable of alerting their owners when a telephone rings or someone comes to the front door; others are trained to fetch a profoundly deaf parent when a baby

40

cries, to wake up their owner when an alarm clock goes off or to warn them when a whistling kettle comes to the boil – all things that those of us with good hearing take so much for granted.

THE KENNEL CLUB

1-5 Clarges Street   London W1Y 8AB

When the first dog show was organised at Newcastle Town Hall on 28 June 1859 it attracted sixty entrants, sparking in the British a passion for dogs and exhibitions – a passion that had been signalled by the outstanding success of the Great Exhibition in 1851. Before long dog shows of all sorts, organised and disorganised, were being held around the country. What they lacked was a controlling body and a set of rules that all could abide by, and these were supplied by the twelve gentleman members who set up the Kennel Club in 1873 with the aim of improving pure-bred dogs. They established ten rules for dog shows; if the organisers stuck to them the winning dogs were entered in the Kennel Club stud book. By the end of the century there were nearly thirty major shows and many more smaller shows held annually; in 1985 there were around 7,000! Although it is mainly concerned with the breeding and showing of pure-bred dogs, the Kennel Club does support and lobby for the interests of *all* dogs, pedigree or not.

THE NATIONAL
ANTI-VIVISECTION SOCIETY

51 Harley Street   London W1

According to statistics issued by the National Anti-Vivisection Society, 14,410 experiments were performed on live dogs in 1984. Dogs were subjected to experiments that involved poisoning to test the toxicity of drugs, cosmetics, pesticides and household chemicals; medical tests, including being force-fed with alcohol to see what happened to their livers; and surgical experiments involving the removal of vital organs. At the Ministry of Defence's Porton Down establishment dogs have been dosed with poisonous hydrogen cyanide and used for CS gas tests.

While some of these experiments may be useful, many seem to be pointless and their scientific value very limited. The National Anti-Vivisection Society points out that a number of drugs that had been 'proved' safe by animal experiments later turned out to damage humans. Early attempts at blood transfusions using dogs proved successful, but when the same techniques were applied to humans most of them died – no one had done any investigations into human blood and they didn't know that humans had four blood groups. Relying on animals can be very misleading.

The National Anti-Vivisection Society is particularly concerned about the problem of pets falling into the hands of the laboratories that do such research. In 1981 the *Sheffield Morning Star* reported the case of a family whose pet Labrador went missing. He was rescued when animal activists broke into the research laboratories at Sheffield University and found him there. Dogs may be obtained by replying to adverts in local papers for 'good homes required for unwanted puppies', while others may be stolen in the street and then sold to laboratories and research centres. The NAVS is fighting to prevent this and as well as offering a £500 reward to anyone supplying information leading to the conviction of any person caught stealing and supplying animals for vivisection, it offers these tips to concerned dog-owners:

1 Don't let your dog out alone.

2 If you see anyone trying to make off with your pet, or with other dogs, report it to the police.

3 If you offer puppies for sale, make sure that you know exactly where each one is going and follow it up.

4 If you have a dog that you want to get rid of, never give it to a dealer, who may sell it to a laboratory. The RSPCA, PDSA, and the National Canine Defence League all have animal shelters where dogs can be left without risk and PRO DOGS has a rehoming service which ensures that pets are found suitable new families to live with.

5 If your dog does ever disappear, search for it and then inform the police, the local RSPCA, PDSA, Blue Cross groups and the local vets. Put adverts in the local paper and make an appeal on the local radio, offering a reward.

THE NATIONAL CANINE DEFENCE LEAGUE

1 Pratt Mews   London NW1 0AD

The National Canine Defence League has sixteen rescue centres around the UK in which strays and abandoned dogs are housed with a view to finding new homes for them. Unlike some other dogs' homes it never destroys a dog unless it is so ill that nothing can be done to help it. Many of its dogs find happy new homes with responsible owners, and anyone applying to the NCDL for a dog is expected to go through an interview and prove themselves capable of looking after a dog properly.

For any dog lover who would like to own a dog but for one reason or another can't, they offer a dog sponsoring scheme so that you can have the pleasure of your 'own' dog without having to look after it. Many elderly people worry about what might happen to their dog if they die, and the NCDL offers a service which guarantees that all dogs of deceased owners are well taken care of. On top of all this, the League runs a free advisory service on legal matters concerned with dog ownership, maintains three animal cemeteries and campaigns and advises on all aspects of legislation to do with dogs. For many dog owners membership could prove a very sound investment! Write to the above address for details.

Since it was founded in 1891 the NCDL has awarded medals to humans and dogs who have shown exceptional courage and loyalty in caring for each other. Some of the doggy heroes and heroines are:

Boris, an Alsatian on holiday with his master in Devon when they were marooned on a rock by the incoming tide. Attempts to rescue the owner failed when the rope that was flung to him fell short. Boris jumped into the seething waves, swam to the cliffs, collected the end of the rope and took it back to his master.

Brandy, a drug-sniffing golden retriever who in five years with H.M. Customs and Excise managed to sniff out more than $4 million of hidden cannabis.

Yerba, a six-year-old Alsatian police dog who was shot and killed when he confronted two raiders in August 1984.

Humans who have performed gallant acts on behalf of dogs are awarded Silver Medals for their bravery. Among the medal holders are:

Barbara Boyle, of St Mary Cray, Kent who led fifteen dogs to safety from burning kennels.

Clifford Gray, aged sixteen from Leeds, who rescued a drowning dog from the Leeds-Liverpool Canal.

Stephen Yardman from Hemel Hempstead, who climbed down a steep cliff to save a dog that had been thrown over by its owner and broken its leg.

PRO DOGS

**Rocky Bank   4 New Road   Ditton   Maidstone
Kent ME20 6AD**

PRO DOGS was founded in 1976 by Lesley Scott Ordish in response to a number of anti-dog television programmes and newspaper articles. PRO DOGS' philosophy is, quite simply, that dogs are good for people and that responsible owners and breeders can counter criticism in a positive way. PRO DOGS is supported by a panel of highly-qualified professionals who supply accurate information to support the canine cause, and by 30,000 dog-owners organised in 30 branches throughout the country. To join, write to the address above with a stamped addressed envelope.

Among its campaigns has been one to end the practice of electrocuting dogs, a method used throughout the country and at the Dogs Home Battersea until the evidence supplied by PRO DOGS convinced those in charge that it was cruel. In 1986 it launched the Better British Breeders service, designed to reduce the number of unwanted and abandoned dogs. Breeders who belong to the scheme adopt a voluntary code of practice, which includes providing a high standard of care for the puppies they breed and taking a long-term responsibility for them. If an owner who buys a dog from a Better British Breeder finds that for one reason or another they cannot keep it, the breeder will take it back and find a new home for it. If you would like to buy a dog from a caring breeder, PRO DOGS can put you in touch with one; write to the address above.

PAT, which stands for PRO DOGS Active Therapy, is a dog visiting scheme launched nationally by PRO DOGS in 1983. Owners of gentle, friendly dogs take their pets to visit local nursing homes, hospitals and institutions so that the people living in them can have the pleasure of their company.

Many elderly people have to leave their pets behind when they enter an institution; stroking and talking to a PAT dog can be a great comfort to them. The Royal College of Nursing has recognised this, and so have many health authorities. PAT dogs have to be tested for temperament and registered before they can start work, and they are in great demand. If you have a calm dog that appreciates lots of attention and you are prepared to make a regular visit to a local home or hospital, contact PRO DOGS for further information about the PAT scheme.

Each year PRO DOGS awards Gold Medals to three exceptional dogs for Lifesaving, Devotion to Duty and Pet of the Year. If you would like to nominate a dog for any of these awards, send full details to PRO DOGS.

LIFESAVING: **Harvey**, a basset hound who saved his owner's family when fire broke out in their home.

DEVOTION TO DUTY: **Favour**, the first Hearing Dog for the Deaf, who has travelled around the country promoting the charity.

PET OF THE YEAR: **Schnorbitz**, the St Bernard belonging to TV celebrity Bernie Winters.

THE ROYAL SOCIETY FOR THE PREVENTION OF CRUELTY TO ANIMALS

Causeway   Horsham   West Sussex RH12 1HG

The RSPCA deals with more dogs than any other animal organisation in this country. Its dog wardens and officers care for many thousands of dogs. In 1985 they found new homes for 51,778, but still had to destroy 52,089. But perhaps the Society's most important work is its prosecution of cruel owners and its campaigns against such things as dog-fighting. In 1985 992 people were found guilty of cruelty to dogs and many were banned from ever owning one again. It's to the RSPCA that most people turn if they suspect someone of cruelty to animals, and if you should witness an incident that needs reporting, the RSPCA offers the following advice.

1 If you can step in and stop it immediately without endangering yourself, then do so.
2 If you have a camera at hand or some other means of recording evidence then use it. If anyone witnesses the incident with you, make sure that you have their name and address.
3 Phone your nearest RSPCA Inspectorate Centre. You'll find the number listed under Royal Society for the Prevention of Cruelty to Animals or in the Yellow Pages under the section headed Animal Welfare. Try to give the details as calmly and objectively as possible.
4 Be prepared to become involved in any legal proceedings that arise. To prosecute someone for cruelty the RSPCA needs witnesses and unless people are prepared to become involved with a case there may be little the organisation can do about it.

SEARCH AND RESCUE DOG ASSOCIATION

c/o Alison Graham   Gwynne Hart & Assocs.
4 Bedford Square   London WC1B 3RA

In 1963 Hamish Macinnes, leader of the Glencoe Mountain Rescue Team, became interested in the use of dogs to help find people who had gone missing in the mountains. He trained his own two Alsatians with such success that the following year a pilot scheme for a further six dogs and handlers was started and in 1965 he founded the Search and Rescue Dog Association. There are now separate Associations for England, Scotland, Wales and Ireland.

The dogs participate in several training courses each year, learning to search out climbers and walkers in all kinds of locations, from rocky crags to open moorland; they also learn to detect people buried by avalanches, though in this country avalanches are rare. A number of breeds, mainly collies, Labradors and Alsatians, are put through the two-year training before becoming search dogs and going out with their handlers as part of rescue teams. In 1986 there were 45 incidents during which English and Scottish dogs were called out; in four of those cases it was the dogs who found the missing people. Among those rescued were two boys suffering from exposure on a Dartmoor marsh and a group of walkers in the Lake District. Yet another example of how dogs can be good for people!

THE INCREDIBLE
ADVENTURES OF BUNGEY

During the reign of James I there was a vogue among dog-lovers for writing the biographies of their remarkable pets. Most remarkable of all was Bungey, a large, shaggy dog, perhaps a cross between a setter and a spaniel, who belonged to Sir John Harington, a godson of Queen Elizabeth I. The only existing picture of Bungey is an illustration of him on the title pages of his master's translation of *Orlando Furioso*, but his good deeds and strange feats were known to many.

Among the most impressive was the way in which he played postman. Carrying a satchel of letters around his neck he made his own way from Bath to Greenwich, where he delivered his messages to Harington's friends and then waited for replies before setting off home again or on to one of his master's other homes. He showed his true worth when he was set the task of carrying two bottles of sherry from Bath to one of Harington's houses. Halfway there the straps which held one of the bottles to him began to come loose. he carefully hid the bottle in some rushes, delivered the other and then returned to collect the one which had come loose.

So admired was he for these feats that Bungey was stolen by the Spanish ambassador. It was six weeks before Harington discovered what had happened to him and went to claim his dog, but no one in the ambassador's household would believe that Bungey belonged to him. Eventually Harington put him through his paces, sending him into the dining hall to collect a pheasant from a dish and then making him return it. At the sight of such obedience the Spanish were reluctantly forced to admit that Sir John *was* Bungey's master and the pair were reunited.

HIS MASTER'S VOICE

As a child I used to love HMV records – and not so much for the music that came from them but for the label, with its little white dog listening intently to the sound of his master's voice coming from the gramophone horn. No other record label held the same charm, and it's all the more charming when one appreciates the story behind the scene.

The little dog in the picture was a black-and-white fox terrier called Nipper. He was adopted by artist Francis Barraud who owned a phonograph with a big black horn, and he used to sit, enraptured, listening to the sounds which came from it. Barraud was so taken by the scene that he painted it, but the black horn of the phonograph made it look very sombre and dull. What he really needed, he decided, was one of the bright brass horns used on the new machines sold by the Gramophone Company. He wasn't able to afford to buy one, so he went along to the company headquarters, explained the situation and asked if he might borrow one. The Gramophone Company was intrigued and they asked him to let them see the finished picture. When he showed it to them they immediately recognised how popular it might be and snapped it up for £50, with another £50 to purchase the copyright.

Barraud must have kicked himself for selling the rights, for Nipper was used all over the world to advertise HMV products – everywhere except those Muslim countries where dogs are considered unclean; in those countries the HMV symbol was a snake. Nipper died in 1895, soon after the picture was completed, but his image was reproduced for more than fifty years on everything from record labels to stained glass windows, statues, and table cruets and Barraud spent the rest of his life making copies of the original for record company executives. In 1954 the world experienced the biggest Nipper of all time when a billboard 25 feet high and bearing his image was erected in New York.

DOGS IN DRAMA

Dogs are mentioned in several of Shakespeare's plays but the only one who gets a name and appears on stage is Crab in *The Two Gentlemen of Verona*, who makes a mess under the table. Shakespeare was only being sensible – every performer is well aware that working with animals and children is just courting disaster. In the London run of a play called *Serena Blandish*, the actress Constance Collier had to make a dramatic stage entrance leading two large greyhounds. She waited with the dogs behind the door through which they were to enter, murmuring to them and preparing them for the moment the door opened and they walked on. When their cue came the dogs were ready all right. The door was flung back and they raced off, as if they were leaving a racing trap, dragging Miss Collier behind them across the stage and out through the nearest exit – which happened to be the fireplace . . .

Another anecdote with both doggy and theatrical overtones involves Noël Coward and Richard Olivier, the young son of Sir Laurence Olivier and Joan Plowright. Coward was visiting the Oliviers at their home in Brighton when Richard asked him what two dogs, in plain view on the seafront, were doing. It was perfectly obvious that they were mating, but Coward tactfully explained, 'It's like this, dear boy: the one in front is blind and the kind one behind is pushing him all the way to St Dunstan's.'

DOGS ON ICE

The Victorian passion for taxidermy extended to pets, and many a lap-dog or favourite hound was stuffed so that its owner could keep it around the house even after its death. One of the most famous stuffed dogs was Barry, the St Bernard who saved forty people from the snows of the St Bernard Pass in Switzerland. After two years in retirement he died in 1815 and was stuffed and put on display. According to a number of taxidermists contacted recently, it's quite rare these days to be asked to stuff a pet. The prices for a professional job are too high for most pet owners to consider it – around £200 for a small dog and £600 or more for an Alsatian!

Of course you don't have to resort to taxidermy to preserve your pet; you can have it frozen or even freeze-dried. A Los Angeles lady, Nola Hudson, is so convinced that in a few years' time cures will be found for most major illnesses that she has had the bodies of her husband and her two Yorkshire terriers deep-frozen.

Another California pet lover has gone one better and had her Pekingese freeze-dried. Now the deceased pet enjoys an eternal snooze on a coffee table in her owner's living-room.

DICKENS'S DOGS

Charles Dickens loved dogs and included many in his novels. In real life his favourite was a white spaniel called Timber Doodle which was presented to him in New York in 1842. Dickens taught him tricks and took him everywhere he went. Many writers have included dogs in their novels, but few have given them such character as Dickens. Here are just a few of his dogs.

Ponto was a pointer whose remarkable skills were described by his owner, Mr Jingles, in *The Pickwick Papers*. Mr Jingles was out for a walk with his dog and climbed a stile into an enclosure to do some shooting. He whistled Ponto to follow but he wouldn't – he'd seen the sign reading, 'Gamekeeper has orders to shoot all dogs found in enclosure' which his master had missed.

Bull's Eye was Bill Sikes's bull terrier in *Oliver Twist*. He was as wicked as his master, and he came to the same horrifying end when he fell from a burning building and was killed.

Jip was Dora Spenlow's small black spaniel in *David Copperfield*. He was a vicious little thing, always barking and yapping; the first time David approaches him he snarls and barks. As a party trick he would get up on the dining table while everyone was eating and walk the length of it, putting his feet in the salt and butter as he went.

Diogenes was a scruffy, gruff mongrel who appeared in *Dombey and Son*. He befriended the lonely Paul Dombey and his sister Florence.

FIVE LOYAL DOGS

Dogs are the most loyal of all pets – though sometimes I have doubts about Rabbit. A plate of smoked salmon and a dog chew and he's anyone's! Here are five of the most loyal dogs on record, though if you have a dog of your own, you may want to add its name to the list.

Gelert One of the best-known folk tales in Wales is the story of Prince Llywellyn and Gelert, his faithful hound. Llywellyn had a palace at Beddgelert in a beautiful valley not far from Snowdon, and he spent much time hunting in the area. One day he called his dogs for the day's hunt but his swiftest and most faithful hound, Gelert, did not come. Llywellyn went off without him. When he returned later Gelert came racing out to meet him, his paws and teeth dripping with blood. The prince was suspicious and raced to the nursery where his one-year-old son slept. The child's cradle was overturned and spattered with blood and the baby was nowhere to be seen. In fury the prince struck Gelert with his sword and pierced his heart.

As the dog gave its final howl Llywellyn heard the baby cry, and lifting the toppled cradle found his son safe beneath it and beside him the body of a wolf, killed by the brave Gelert. Full of remorse, the prince carried the body of his faithful dog out of the castle and buried it in a public place so that everyone would know how brave and loyal Gelert had been.

The only problem with this wonderful story is that not a word of it is true! Beddgelert exists, and so does Gelert's grave, which is visited by thousands of tourists each year. Unfortunately the grave was built less than 200 years ago as a publicity stunt by David Pritchard, landlord of the Royal Goat Inn. He knew an ancient legend about a man who killed his dog by mistake and wove around it the story of Gelert – and one of the earliest advertising cons was born!

Hachiko Hachiko the Akita dog became famous for his loyalty in the early part of this century. Each morning he would accompany his master, Dr Eisaburo Ueno, to the Shibuya railway station near Tokyo and be there to meet him when he returned each evening. Then one day Dr Ueno, who taught at Tokyo University, died at work. Hachiko waited at the station until midnight. Next day, and almost every day for the next nine years, he returned and staged his vigil. When he died in 1934 he was famed throughout Japan and a statue was erected to his memory at the spot on the station where he had sat and waited. Each year since then a remembrance ceremony has been held to commemorate his exceptional loyalty.

Greyfriars Bobby Bobby was a shaggy little Skye terrier who worked with a shepherd called John Grey. In 1858 Grey died and was buried in Greyfriars Churchyard, Edinburgh. The day after the funeral, Bobby was found asleep on his master's grave. Night after night, despite attempts to discourage him, he returned, and soon he was living there. At one o'clock each day, when the gun was fired at Edinburgh Castle, he would go for lunch to the local inn where the owner fed him. For fourteen years he kept watch over the grave and attracted admirers from all over Europe. When he died on 14 January 1872 special dispensation was granted so that he could be buried next to his master and a public collection raised enough money for his headstone and a dogs' drinking fountain with a bronze statue of Bobby on top, which still stands in Candlemaker Row.

Argus was the faithful old hound of Odysseus; he was left behind when his master embarked on his ten-year adventure chronicled in the *Iliad* and the *Odyssey*. Odysseus arrived home in disguise and Argus was the only member of the household who recognised him. The poor old dog only just had time to wag his tail before he died, his life's ambition of seeing his master again fulfilled.

Lord Byron loved dogs, but he was just one of many people to marvel at Argus's fidelity. In *Don Juan* he pictures the situation most men would find at home after an absence of ten years.

> The odds are that he finds a handsome urn
> To his memory – and two or three young misses
> Born to some friend, who holds his wife and riches; –
> And that *his* Argus bites him by – the breeches.

Roquet Legend has it that in the fourteenth century a French-born healer called Roch went to Italy to nurse the sick during a plague. In Piacenza he, too, was struck down and crawled into the woods to die where he would avoid infecting others. There he was found by Roquet, a nobleman's hound, who each day brought him a loaf of bread and licked his sores until Roch recovered. Later the healer was canonised as St Roche, and today in some Roman Catholic parishes dogs are blessed on his feast day, August 16th.

DOG
DIRECTORY

FIVE CANINE MOVIE STARS

Rin Tin Tin the Alsatian was the most famous of all dog movie stars. As a puppy he was rescued from an abandoned German dugout in France by American airmen. He was taken back to the USA and trained for the police, but his good looks and obedience were spotted by Warner Brothers. His first movie, *Where the North Begins* (1923) made him a celebrity. In 1925 he was voted the most popular star in America by one poll of cinema audiences and he went on to make more than forty films, earn $1,000,000 and keep Warner Brothers solvent during a difficult period. On the film set a suite of rooms was kept reserved for him and he had his own chauffeur and cook to ensure that he was well looked after. At the height of his popularity he was receiving 10,000 letters a week from devoted fans – more than Douglas Fairbanks Junior, though not as many as Mickey Mouse. On set he was usually very well-behaved and he had an instinctive understanding of what the director required him to do – but he did occasionally bite his co-stars. Actor Charles Hargan, who often did fight scenes with Rin Tin Tin, was once bitten on the leg during a filmed tussle. He bit the movie star on the ear, hard, and Rin Tin Tin never nipped him again. When he died in 1932 the star's job was taken by his son, Rin Tin Tin Junior.

Lassie was the other great dog star. In Eric Knight's novel *Lassie Come Home* Lassie was a bitch. For the films a rough collie dog called Pal took the part and earned $250 per week. He appeared in seven movies and also, most remarkably, on a radio show, where he was required to whine and bark on cue. From 1954–73 four generations of his family, all male, appeared in the Lassie TV series and his great-great-great grandson starred in the last movie, *The Magic of Lassie*, in 1978.

Rover was the world's first canine movie star. His real name was Blair and he belonged to Cecil Hepworth, the man who made the seven-minute film *Rescued by Rover* for £7 13s 9d in 1905. In it Rover rescued a baby, played by Hepworth's own child, from gypsies; it was very much a home movie in the pioneering days of film. It was also an overnight success and so many copies were ordered that the negative fell apart. Fortunately Rover remembered his role and the whole film was reshot twice to satisfy public demand. Rover went on to star in seven more films before his death in 1914.

Bullet was the Alsatian companion of cowboy star Roy Rogers and his horse Trigger throughout the 1950s. When he died he was stuffed and put on display next to Trigger, who also suffered the same fate, at the Dale Evans Museum in California.

Benji started life in a Californian animal sanctuary and ended up being *the* canine star of the 1970s. A shaggy, appealing mongrel, his film debut was in *Benji* in 1974 in which he saved two children. The film was particularly memorable because it was shot largely at a height of eighteen inches from the ground so that the action was seen from the dog's point of view. By the time a sequel came round he was seventeen years old and couldn't take the part, so his daughter stepped in for *For the Love of Benji*. In America the films were extremely popular and both Benjis made personal appearances and gave television interviews.

ALSO APPEARING . . .

Not quite stars in their own right, these are the canine performers you may know well by sight but not by name.

Asta was the schnauzer bitch in Dashiell Hammett's book *The Thin Man*. In the film based on the book she was played by a wirehaired fox terrier called Skippy.

Goofy One of Walt Disney's most famous dogs, he started life with the name Dippy Dawg before establishing himself as Mickey Mouse's best friend.

Duke A Great Dane who starred alongside cowboy hero Tom Mix.

K9 Dr Who's mechanical canine companion who survived many adventures in space. K9 obviously had terrier origins.

Laughing Gravy was Laurel and Hardy's mongrel.

Pongo was the father of the fifteen puppies stolen by Cruella de Vil who wanted to turn them into coats in Dodie Smith's story (and Walt Disney's film) *One Hundred and One Dalmatians*.

Rowlf is the shaggy dog with floppy ears who plays the piano in Jim Henson's famous *Muppet Show*. He was first created in the 1960s and only later became leader of the Muppet Orchestra. He is reported not to like playing Offenbach.

Scraps A great favourite of Charlie Chaplin, with whom he starred in *A Dog's Life* in 1918. Chaplin had almost given up looking for the right dog when Scraps jumped into his lap; a star was born and he went on to appear in a series of more than fifty films during which time he saved countless men, women and children from a variety of predicaments.

Strongheart was an ex-Red Cross dog who'd served in the trenches during World War I and was trained as a police dog on his return. He was a stunningly intelligent animal and would 'act' to order, changing his expression when given instructions. The only thing he didn't like doing was howling. If a scene required him to howl he would be depressed for several days afterwards. Eventually a double was supplied to do this undignified work for him. Strongheart was the first dog to play a guide dog on screen.

Toto was the doggy star of *The Wizard of Oz*; he played Judy Garland's pet. In the original book by L. Frank Baum he hurt his teeth while trying to bite the Tin Woodman.

DISNEY'S DOGS

Walt Disney's animated films starred a number of dogs, but the most famous of all are the Dalmatian stars of *One Hundred and One Dalmatians*. Not so well known is the fact that he did careful research into all the animals he portrayed on film. When he wanted to show Dalmatians, which were at the time uncommon in the USA, he went to France to visit a French titled lady, the Comtesse de Quelen, who owned a family of the spotty dogs. There he filmed them from all angles and in all actions to make sure that he and his artists got the shape, movements and markings of the dogs absolutely right. The results, which are very accurate, can be seen for themselves, and the film was so popular that soon everyone wanted a Dalmatian. Within months the price of spotted puppies had risen 400%.

THIRTEEN NATIONAL DOGS

Most of these dogs are recognised as the national dog, or in some cases the national symbol, of their country.

1. America – Boston terrier, bred for dog-fighting in the dog-fighting capital of the USA.
2. Belgium – Schipperke and the four breeds of Belgian shepherd dog; Groenendael, Tervueren, Malinois and Laekenois.
3. Britain – the British bulldog.
4. Finland – the Finnish spitz, very common in Finland but rarely found elsewhere.
5. France – the poodle or the briard, the shaggy French sheepdog.
6. Germany – the German shepherd or the dachshund.
7. Holland – the keeshond, which is a Dutch symbol of resistance against William of Orange.
8. Hungary – the Vizsla, the smooth-coated hunting dog rare outside its native country.
9. Ireland – the Kerry blue or the Irish setter.
10. Japan – the Akita.
11. Russia – the borzoi, so beloved of the Tsar and the Russian aristocracy that in the years leading up to the revolution it was reported that the dog had been spoiled and could no longer catch wolves.
12. Scotland – the deerhound, so prized that after the Battle of Culloden only the Highland Chieftains were allowed to own them.
13. Wales – the corgi.

DOGS IN SPACE

The first living creature to orbit the earth was Laika, nicknamed 'Little Lemon' or 'Curly'. She was an 11-pound Samoyed husky bitch and she was launched into space on 3 November 1957 on board Sputnik II, wired into a special air-conditioned chamber so that scientists could monitor the physiological effects of the flight on her. She seemed to cope with the experience well, but because the technology of the time did not allow scientists to bring back the spacecraft in one piece she died after ten days when her oxygen supply gave out.

On a happier note, Belka and Strelka became the first two animals to survive an orbital space flight. Like the first dog in space they were Samoyed huskies, and they were launched in Sputnik V on 19 August 1960. After twenty-five hours, during which they circled the earth seventeen times, they landed safely. They'd suffered no apparent harm and both later had normal litters of puppies; in fact one of Strelka's puppies was given as a gift to President John F. Kennedy's wife, Jackie.

FOUR SKY DOGS

The Aurora Borealis In Eskimo tradition the shimmering lights of the Aurora Borealis are teams of dogs carrying the souls of the dead from earth on sleds.

Cynosure The word cynosure means 'the centre of attraction', and it has come to be the name for the Pole Star, which is seen by everyone. The name Cynosure comes from the Greek for 'dog tail'.

Sirius is the Dog Star, the brightest star in the heavens, which appears in the Canis Major constellation. The ancient Egyptians calculated their calendars by it because when it rose in the sky it meant that it was time for the Nile to flood and restore the fertility of the land. In many other civilisations, however, Sirius was despised. It rises at dawn in the hottest months of the year, July and August, which were also the worst times for plague, drought and famine. To the Greeks it was the 'evil star' and in this country too it had a bad reputation. The saying 'dog days', meaning a bad, malignant time, refers to the hot months when Sirius rises at dawn and dogs grow fractious in the heat and are more inclined to bite.

T'ien Kow is the Celestial Dog of Chinese mythology who causes eclipses by eating the sun. In an effort to scare him off and prevent the eclipse, which they feared, people would beat drums and bang gongs.

THE YEAR OF THE DOG

The Chinese horoscope is based on twelve animal signs – the rat, buffalo, tiger, cat, dragon, snake, horse, goat, monkey, rooster, dog and pig. Unlike the astrological horoscope, in which all twelve signs of the zodiac occur every year, each Chinese sign occurs in a twelve-year cycle and lasts for a year. It's the year in which you are born that determines your Chinese animal sign and if you were born in 1910, 1922, 1934, 1946, 1958, 1970 or 1982 you are a Dog.

THE DOG CHARACTER

People born in the year of the Dog have a very strong sense of fair play and duty and justice. They're generally not too concerned with making a lot of money or amassing possessions for themselves; instead they pour their energy into trying to make the world a better place for the disadvantaged. Suffering attracts the Dog, who is anxious to help and right wrongs, and the Dog friend will stick with you through thick and thin.

Like all dogs, they are happiest when they feel needed and

when there is something for them to do. If you have a friend who always helps out in a crisis and even seems to thrive on it, it's likely that he or she is a Dog. Dogs keep their promises and once committed to a task stick to it with dogged determination until they've seen it through. They work best if given direction by someone else; like a guide dog or a police dog, they need a partner to give them that little extra confidence that makes them so good at their work. In business or in the office they can be very successful, meticulous and hard-working, particularly if they are part of a partnership or team which backs them up.

On a less happy note, Dogs lack self-confidence and tend to be pessimistic about their chances of success and the world in general. They are sometimes wracked by self-doubt, which can lead to depression. Dogs tend not to be terribly proud or pompous or boastful; they are self-critical and anxious to please, but they do appreciate praise where it is due. A Dog will work hard and put up with a lot from others, but if its loyalty and devotion are met with nothing but harsh words or criticism it will go off in search of someone who shows proper appreciation. Dogs are also obsessed with getting things right and can get bogged down in minor details, losing sight of the major goal.

A Dog's home is usually spick and span, furnished with classic low-key taste. There will be few extravagent items because the Dog doesn't waste money on luxuries or spend a lot of money on himself. Dogs are often to be found in the 'serving' professions – in medicine, nursing, social work, teaching, running charities or even in politics. In their personal lives Dogs are idealists and most partners fall short of their requirements. This can lead to a string of broken marriages (Zsa Zsa Gabor is a Dog) or to no marriages at all.

TEN FAMOUS 'DOGS'

1 Brigitte Bardot – actress, dog-lover and animal rights supporter
2 Alan Bennett – witty, amusing, but retiring writer whose work often includes social criticism and praise of the underdog
3 Judi Dench – actress with strong personal convictions
4 Zsa Zsa Gabor – actress most famous for her string of broken marriages
5 Tony Hancock – brilliant comedian dogged by depression
6 Michael Jackson – pop megastar who lives a reclusive life
7 Jonathan Miller – doctor, philosopher and theatre director: classic thinking Dog
8 Clive Ponting – idealistic civil servant who leaked classified information because he felt it was right
9 Mother Teresa of Calcutta – gave up everything in order to help others
10 Daley Thompson – total, unswerving dedication to his goal

TV STARS

Dougal Shaggy yellow dog of indeterminate breed who starred in *The Magic Roundabout*, always asking silly questions.
Petra The most famous of all *Blue Peter* dogs, Petra made 1,192 appearances on the long-running children's show.

Although she wasn't the most distinguished-looking of dogs – she was a black and tan mongrel – she had her statue cast in bronze and met almost everyone worth knowing, including many members of the royal family and the most famous pop stars of her day.

Roly White standard poodle star of *Eastenders*. He lives in the Queen Vic pub and puts up uncomplainingly with all the ballyhoo in Albert Square.

Schnorbitz Named Pet of the Year by PRO DOGS, Schnorbitz assists comedian Bernie Winters with his act.

Spit Well-known glove puppet-dog who belongs to presenter and comedian Bob Carolgees and is just as disgusting as his name suggests.

Willy Another *Eastenders* star, Willy the pug is owned by Ethel who cleans the Queen Vic. He caused some consternation when he went missing in March 1986 but Detective Sergeant Quick found him.

SEVEN FICTIONAL DOGS

The Hound of the Baskervilles in *The Hound of the Baskervilles* by Sir Arthur Conan Doyle.

Garryowen, a sandy-coloured mongrel in *Ulysses* by James Joyce.

Bevis, a faithful mastiff who serves his owner and saves his life in *Woodstock* by Sir Walter Scott. Possibly based on Scott's own deerhound/mastiff cross Maida, which he idolised.

Bob, a wire-haired terrier given to Hercule Poirot at the end of *Poirot Loses a Client*, probably based on Agatha Christie's own dog, Peter.

Tricki-Woo, a hideously spoilt Pekingese in James Herriot's *All Creatures Great and Small*.

Nana, the canine nanny in *Peter Pan* by J.M. Barrie.

McIntosh, the star of P.G. Wodehouse's *Jeeves and the Dog McIntosh*, an Aberdeen terrier who is given away to the wrong person and has to be stolen back by Jeeves.

THE IRISH WOLFHOUND – A RECONSTRUCTED DOG

The oldest record of the Irish wolfhound goes back an amazing 1,600 years to a letter written by Consul Quintas Aurelius in AD 391, in which he expresses his thanks for a gift of seven of the dogs which had been sent to Rome to appear in the circus and had filled 'all Rome with wonder.' The wolfhound was for many more years a much valued dog. In or around the year 1000 King Myrkjartan of Iceland presented one to the Icelandic hero Gunnar Jarl.

Throughout this time wolves were a serious problem in Britain. They were also very difficult to catch and a wolf hunt could take a long time. In an attempt to ensure that something was done Anglo-Saxon kings sentenced criminals to hunt them as a punishment and imposed a wolf tax on the Welsh, who were requested to supply a given quota of dead wolves to prove that they were doing their bit. This prompted one Welsh king to report to his English overlord that he had killed every wolf there was in Wales. It turned out to be one of the earliest recorded attempts to fool the tax man, but it wasn't so very long before all these efforts paid off and the wolf disappeared from this country. With nothing left to hunt, the wolfhound quickly declined in numbers and was declared extinct by the middle of the last century.

At this point Captain George Graham of Dursley, Gloucestershire, stepped in and started the task of recreating these huge hounds. He gathered the few wolfhound specimens he could still find, read all he could about the ancient original wolfhounds and began reconstructing the breed using deerhounds and Great Danes. So well did he succeed that the Irish wolfhound is once again an established and prized breed – though how much resemblance it bears to its ancient ancestors, no one knows for certain.

THE DOGS OF WAR

ANCIENT TIMES

Since ancient times man has taken dogs to war both to fight and to act as guard. The most famous and feared dogs of all were the British mastiffs, huge ferocious dogs, ancestors of today's mastiff, who were let loose in the front ranks of armies and raced ahead to scatter and terrify the enemy. The war dogs of the Gauls, imported into France from Britain, struck fear into the hearts of even the Romans. Pliny the Younger wrote that some of these dogs were trained to move across the battlefields in platoons, never retreating until they were given the command. One of the reasons for Julius Caesar's invasion of Britain was to get his hands on some of these amazing beasts and send them back to Rome, where they were greeted with awed admiration for the way in which they could kill a bull with a single bite.

During medieval times some dogs went into battle wearing full coats of armour. Others were more lightly clad, with just a broad collar protecting their jugular veins and an identity tag with the name of their owner and his coat of arms. While some dogs were employed in direct battle, others were taken along as protection. One of a war dog's duties was to stand over his master if he lay dead or wounded and protect the body from attack by other dogs, soldiers or scavenging wolves.

A Welsh tale tells the story of a battle between the Welsh and the army of Henry II (1133–89), during which a young Welshman was killed. His greyhound stood over his body for eight days without food or water, refusing to allow anyone else near. Although the English detested the Welsh they recognised a good dog when they saw one and, for the animal's sake, buried the rapidly-decomposing body. It's no wonder that so many medieval tombs show knights resting with dogs at their feet. Although dogs were generally despised during this period of history, a faithful and devoted hound was a knight's best friend in battle.

WORLD WAR I

Bearing in mind the early success of British war dogs, it's perhaps something of a surprise to learn that when World War I broke out Germany had 6,000 dogs trained for work and we had one, a solitary Airedale guard dog. It wasn't until 1916, when thousands of men had been killed delivering messages on the front, that the War Office finally agreed to give dogs a go and the first dog training school was set up at Shoeburyness, Essex.

Dogs were brought from animal shelters to be trained and hundreds were donated by members of the public. In a letter accompanying her pet, one child wrote, 'We have let Daddy go and fight the Kaiser, now we are sending Jack to do his bit.' Within days of being sent from their comfortable family homes the canine recruits were in training, learning not to flinch as grenades exploded around them and being taught to deliver messages over ever-increasing distances to a handler who soon became their master.

Only a month later the dogs found themselves in the middle of the fighting on the front line. They were kept there by soldiers who ensured that they were well-watered but hungry. If a message needed to be sent back to HQ the note was inserted in a small can attached to the dog's collar and it was let loose to go tearing across the battlefield, leaping trenches, skirting shell holes and speeding back to where it knew its handler and dinner were waiting. Dog messengers were three times faster than their human equivalent, and because they moved more quickly and presented a smaller target, more messages arrived safely. Unfortunately, as Jilly Cooper makes clear in her book *Animals in War*, some people refused to believe that dogs could be of use and dozens of specially trained animals were ignored or shot by officers – tragic when one considers that many of them were much-loved pets who had been volunteered in the first place.

Other dogs were called up to pull gun carriages, charging across the battlefield with their load and racing off to safety as soon as they were released, or to carry packs of grenades or lay telegraph wires across open stretches where a man would be instantly killed. The Italians used larger breeds to take supplies across the Alps. Dogs could scramble up rock faces where no mule could go and as a reward for their efforts they received the same rations as the soldiers, including coffee and bread for breakfast and meat, bread and chocolate for supper. Even the smallest dog had his uses; terriers were kept in trenches to catch the plagues of rats that feasted on human corpses. In all around 7,000 dogs from Britain gave their lives, and in doing so they saved those of many men.

For one breed, the Bouvier des Flandres, World War I almost brought extinction. An intelligent and obedient herd dog, it was called up in large numbers for messenger and ambulance work. Most were killed but an army vet saved the breed with the help of a single dog, Nic, who is the ancestor of every modern Bouvier des Flandres. These days they are recognised as making excellent police and army dogs.

WORLD WAR II

Britain was once more caught on the hop when World War II broke out. Arguing that these were modern times and that machines had replaced the work done by dogs, the War Office was again reluctant to invest in canine recruits. Once again, it was recognised too late that dogs could do what no man or machine was capable of and the Army War Dog School opened in Potters Bar.

Alsatians were trained as guard dogs and patrol dogs, whose job it was to guide small patrols of soldiers across no man's land and silently warn of approaching enemies. A new development were mine dogs, who proved more effective than any mechanical metal detector when it came to sniffing out buried explosives. Until this time it had been believed that dogs were only capable of detecting a substance buried at a maximum depth of sixteen inches, but the mine dogs proved that their noses were far more sensitive than that. *And* they could detect mines constructed from plastic, wood and glass, which was more than could be said for any metal detector. Despite the dangers of the work most of them loved every minute of it, particularly the praise they received each time they found a mine.

Services other than the army found a use for dogs. Many ships kept a dog, whose acute hearing could provide early warning of air raids and, particularly in the Far East, warn of pirates. The SAS and Parachute regiment dropped 'paradogs' who gamely jumped out of planes without hesitation and, once back on the ground, guarded their human comrades. Back home in blitzed London amateur dogs were helping to locate the dead and injured among the rubble. Many dogs had no training and needed none – instinct was enough and they saved many lives.

In Russia, in a last attempt to stop the German tanks that were heading towards Moscow, hundreds of dogs were trained to go on suicide missions. Each equipped with a primed bomb strapped on its back, they were trained to dash across open ground and crouch under enemy tanks until the inevitable explosion. They, and all the other dogs who so unquestioningly played small but vital parts in the war, will not be forgotten.

VC WINNERS

The Dickin Medal was instituted by the People's Dispensary for Sick Animals and is awarded to creatures who show exceptional bravery in dangerous circumstances, which is why it is known as the 'animals' VC'. Here are ten canine heroes who won the right to wear it.

Beauty, Irma, Rex, Thorn and Jet These five, four Alsatians and Beauty the wire-haired fox terrier, saved hundreds of lives during the Blitz by sniffing out survivors under rubble. Irma could distinguish between live and dead casualties. She would walk over the rubble and if she sensed a survivor beneath, would bark. If she knew she'd found a corpse she would merely given a quick wag of her tail to indicate its location.

Bob was a crossbred collie who went with the 6th Queen's Own Royal West Kent Regiment to North Africa. He won his medal in 1943 after leading a night patrol into enemy lines. (His white patches were painted out to improve his camouflage on such occasions.) Just when the patrol wanted to push forward, Bob froze and refused to budge. Ignoring his warning the soldiers crept on – and came across an enemy patrol only a couple of hundred yards ahead. Having been forewarned they were able to retreat silently, but only after collecting valuable information.

Ricky The most famous of all the mine dogs, Ricky was a charmingly scruffy Welsh sheepdog who was sniffing out explosives planted on a Dutch canal bank when a mine blew up several feet away, killing an officer and wounding Ricky in the face. He calmly continued with his work. Ricky had been volunteered by his owner and after the war the army offered a large sum for him, so desperate were they to keep him. The owner, who had missed his brave dog, said no.

Rifleman Khan Khan, an Alsatian, took part in the 1944 assault on the Dutch island of Walcheren. He was approaching the shore with his handler under fire when their boat capsized. Khan swam to shore but couldn't find his handler, Corporal Muldoon, who, it transpired, was a non-swimmer. Khan plunged back in and, dodging the shells, began to search for his drowning master. He found him in the nick of time and towed him to shore.

Rip was a homeless, starving mongrel who was given shelter by the Poplar ARP wardens and eventually adopted as their mascot. In gratitude for their help (half a million homeless dogs had already been put down) he started sniffing out casualties trapped in buildings. During his service with the ARP he found dozens of people.

Rob was a black and white mongrel who made more than twenty parachute jumps with the SAS. He was dropped into North Africa and Italy, and it was his job to guard his fellow soldiers during their dangerous sorties. He was once dropped behind enemy lines and stayed there undercover for months.

MASCOTS

Unlike the trained war dogs, mascots simply existed to give comfort and luck to their company. While they were doing so, many proved themselves heroes too . . .

1 **Billy** was a bull terrier who travelled with the Royal Ulster Rifles for fifteen years. He went through the Boer War with them too, and on days when they rode as much as fifty miles he would purposely put on a limp and hobble along in a pitiful way until someone offered him a lift on a horse.

2 **Bobby** Bobby's moment of fame came at the Battle of Maiwand in 1880, during the Afghan War, when his entire battalion was wiped out and he was captured. Eventually released, he returned with the remains of the regiment to England where he was presented to Queen Victoria dressed in a red velvet coat. Her Majesty was much taken with this little white mongrel and it was reported that when she heard that he had died after being run over by a hansom cab she shed some tears for him.

3 **Bud** was a bull terrier smuggled into France with the 82nd Division of the 325th Machine Gun Company. After he had been gassed on the Somme a special mask was made for him. He learned to lie flat when shells came over, made himself useful as a ratter and survived the war alongside his master. When he died in America at the age of thirteen he was given a military burial in a war cemetery.

4 **Judy** A liver-and-white pedigree pointer, Judy served as

mascot on a number of ships in and around the China Sea. She was torpedoed and sunk twice, captured by the Japanese twice and survived in two prison camps despite being condemned to death on a number of occasions. Her contribution to the morale of the men condemned to build the Sumatran railway was summed up in a poem written by an unknown soldier:

> They would stagger to their work place
> Though they really ought to die.
> And would mutter in their beards
> If that bitch can, so can I.

After three-and-a-half years in the camps she and her master Frank Williams were liberated and came back to England, where Judy received a Dickin medal for her bravery and a life pension and made a guest appearance on the *In Town Tonight* TV show.

5 Rats was a famous mongrel who served with the Grenadier Guards, Queen's Own Highlanders and Welsh Guards in Northern Ireland. If ever proof were needed of the toughness of mongrels, Rats' story would suffice. During his years of service he was shot, burned – he lost several inches from the end of his tail – blown up and run over. He was involved in many car chases, took helicopter rides (and once jumped thirty feet from one) and was an IRA target. The ultimate morale booster for troops abroad, he was eventually retired in 1980.

6 Scout served with the 1st Royal Dragoons during the Boer War and was best-known for the way in which she ran ahead of the regiment barking at everything she saw. She died in India in 1904 and had been buried for two days before it was decided to dig her up and stuff her. Unfortunately the Indian taxidermist made such a mess of her that poor Scout was buried again.

BURGLAR-PROOF

In a 1985 survey of 300 convicted criminals, many admitted that dogs were top of their list of burglar deterrents and that they wouldn't attempt to break into a house if there was a dog on the premises.

You might imagine that most of them were worried about Alsatians and Dobermanns, but also high on the list of burglars' pet hates are small yapping dogs. A burglar in Stratford-upon-Avon was caught after being backed into a corner by two determined Tibetan terriers, both under ten inches tall, and an intruder who broke into a house in Southend had his ankles savaged by a Yorkshire terrier. It's not so surprising when you realise that these small breeds, now thought of mainly as lap-dogs, were once hardy hunters in their own right. The dachshund has been used throughout history for hunting deer and badgers; the Yorkshire terrier, these days often seen with a bow in its hair, was once a champion ratter, much prized by northern miners for its aggression and willingness to tackle anything!

THE VALIANT NEWFOUNDLAND

During the eighteenth century it was a common occurrence during a Newfoundland winter to see a couple of huge, shaggy, immensely strong dogs pulling a cart or sled for several miles. The dogs were so reliable and intelligent they didn't even need a driver and would find their own way to their destination. In the summer the dogs were taken on board the fishing boats where they served as guards and life-savers, happily jumping over the side to retrieve lost equipment and even lost fishermen.

So docile and helpful were these dogs that soon English sailors adopted them and by the middle of the century Newfoundlands, as they were called, had something of a cult. In France, too, their qualities as life-savers were appreciated and a whole corps of them were stationed along the banks of the Seine in Paris to haul out people who fell in. One of them became famous for his over-zealous attitude to work; he used to pull out people who were enjoying themselves taking a pleasant swim.

Throughout the following century they grew in number and in reputation. During a performance of a play called *Jesse Vere* at a Woolwich theatre the actor playing the villain had to abduct the young heroine. As he grabbed her a Newfoundland among the audience decided to come to her aid and leapt at the unfortunate actor. It took several people to drag the dog away. Up in Scotland an enterprising gentleman used to send his two dogs to collect his post and bread each morning. Without any human guide they would pull their special cart to the bakery where newly-baked bread would be put in a lockable compartment, and then head for home, stopping at the Post Office for letters on their way.

But in 1803 there occurred an incident which darkened their reputation. One Colonel Montgomery was out exercising his Newfoundland in Hyde Park when it got into a fight with another belonging to a Captain Macnamara. As they pulled their dogs apart they exchanged a few words, which Macnamara didn't like. He told Montgomery that he'd spoken arrogantly; Montgomery told *him* that if he felt insulted he knew exactly where to find him. The matter escalated, and three hours later the two men fought a duel during which Macnamara was injured and Montgomery killed. As duelling was illegal Macnamara was tried for manslaughter – with the death penalty waiting if he was found guilty. He wasn't, fortunately, but many a Newfoundland owner must have made a silent vow not to let his love for his wonderful pet go to his head.

MAN BITES DOG

It's become a standard piece of advice to aspiring journalists that if a dog bites a man there's no story, but if a man bites a dog – well, that's *news*. The saying 'man bites dog' can be traced back to a poem by Oliver Goldsmith entitled 'Elegy on the Death of a Mad Dog'. It tells the story of a dog that went mad and bit a man and ends with the lines:

> The man recover'd of the bite,
> The dog it was that died.

The poem passed into popular folklore and a number of new versions appeared, including, it's believed, a funny one in which a man *did* bite a dog – hence the advice of editors to their journalists.

FIVE FAVOURITE CARTOON CANINES

Snoopy The most famous beagle in the world! Since he made his debut on 2 October 1950 the *Peanuts* cartoon, featuring Snoopy, has generated syndicated cartoon strips all over the world, books, a TV series, a musical and merchandise from greetings cards to bedlinen. Charles M. Schulz based his famous creation on his own black and white dog Spike, which he was given when he was thirteen.

Gnasher is Dennis the Menace's naughty black dog in *The Beano*. His breed is difficult to guess but probably contains a good deal of terrier (intelligence and aggression), a touch of poodle (his shaggy black coat) and a soupçon of Alsatian (to explain his exceptional loyalty to Dennis).

Scooby Doo is the huge, blustering Great Dane who in each of his television cartoon adventures is proved to be terrified of everything

Fred Basset is the loyal, long-suffering basset hound in the *Daily Mail*'s cartoon.

Snowy is the little white terrier who trots around at the heels of Tintin in the comic strip created by Hergé. He's been everywhere – under the sea in a specially designed wetsuit and in space in his own helmet. In the original French he is called Milou.

THE NOBLE GREYHOUND

The greyhound is one of the most ancient of all breeds. Carvings from Egypt and Assyria dating from around 4,000–3,000 BC show greyhound-like dogs being used for the chase and by the ninth century AD they had been established in Britain by the Romans. The name 'greyhound' probably comes from the Anglo-Saxon word *greg*, meaning dog. When it arrived in this country the greyhound revolutionised the dog world and hunting in particular, because native British dogs lacked the speed and grace of the new breed. British mastiffs were fine for fighting and guard duty (in fact the Romans took many of them back to Rome, where their size and ferocity were considered quite amazing) but it was the greyhound which became the most prized dog of all.

For many centuries they were the dogs of the nobility and they were carefully bred and assessed for their grace and speed. *The Boke of St Albans*, written by Dame Juliana Berners in 1486, includes this description of what a good greyhound should look like:

A greyhounde should be headed lyke a snake,
And neckyd lyke a drake,
Fotyd lyke a cat,
Tayled lyke a ratte,
Syded lyke a bream
And chyned lyke a beam
Then ys greyhounde well y schapte.

Greyhound racing of one sort or another has probably gone on almost on long as there have been greyhounds to race against each other. Charles II held races at Hampton Court, but they didn't really catch on until 1780 when an enterprising Welshman had the bright idea of fastening a stuffed hare to a rope and dragging it along a straight 400-yard course using a windlass. Forty years later someone devised the circular track and patented the idea, but it wasn't put to use for a long time. Then at the turn of the century an Oklahoma farmer, O.P. Smith, revived the idea as an amusement. He was visited by Charles Munn, an Englishman, who was so excited at what he saw that he made films of the races and showed them to Brigadier-General A.C. Critchley, who liked the sport and was mainly responsible for introducing and promoting it in this country. The first English greyhound stadium was built at Bellevue, Manchester and the first greyhound meet held at Wembley stadium in 1927; the sport was an almost immediate success and throughout the 1950s was one of the three most popular spectator sports of the decade.

Probably the most famous racing greyhound of all time was Mick the Miller who won two Derbys and nineteen consecutive races. He was famous on the racetrack for buttering up the audiences, wagging his tail cheerfully at well-attended meets but not bothering if the crowds were thin. When he died he was stuffed and now can be seen on display at the Natural History museum!

TWELVE WORKING BREEDS

There are many breeds of dogs who can round up sheep or keep guard, but some were bred for specific purposes. Here are a dozen of them.

1 **Afghan hound** Bred for hunting gazelle, leopards and jackals.
2 **Borzoi** The borzoi was bred to course wolves on the Russian steppes.
3 **Bulldog** The bulldog was bred for that great British sport, bull-baiting. Until 1850, when baiting was banned, it had longish legs and looked like today's boxer. After the ban the breed went out of fashion, partly because it was very fierce. When a few enthusiasts got together and decided to save it, they created the modern short-legged version of the dog.
4 **Bull mastiff** A mixture of bulldog and mastiff, the bull mastiff came into vogue as a gamekeeper's dog during the nineteenth century. Strong, brave and quiet, gamekeepers used them to help catch poachers at a time when poaching was a hanging offence and if trapped the culprit often tried to kill the keeper. Bull mastiffs were popularly known as Gamekeeper's Night Dogs.
5 **Dalmatian** Throughout the eighteenth century the Dalmatian was *the* fashionable dog in English society. It was used as a carriage dog, ostensibly trotting along behind the carriage to protect the inmates from robbers, but in fact just for decoration.

6 **Elkhounds** Elks being too big for a dog to tackle, the elkhound is trained to track its prey, then bark hard and monotonously to guide the hunter in the correct direction. If the elk moves off the dog follows silently until its stops, then resumes barking.

7 **Fila Brasileiro** This Brazilian dog was originally used in battle to kill Indians, then used for tracking runaway slaves. With the outlawing of slavery they went into decline and were nearly extinct until Brazilian embassies requested them as part of their representation abroad. They are exceptionally ferocious and cannot be handled by anyone except their owner, hence their excellence as watchdogs and their unsuitability for much else.

8 **Great Dane** Originally bred for their strength as war dogs on the battlefield, then used for hunting wild boar. Throughout the seventeenth and eighteenth centuries they were used for pulling dog carts.

9 **Labrador retriever** Originally a fisherman's companion, swimming between fishing boats dragging nets and ropes.

10 **Puffinhound** A dog that climbs steep cliffs and collects puffins' nests and, on occasion, kills and retrieves the birds themselves.

11 **Pyrenean mountain dog** Originally a shepherd's dog, but during the fifteenth century became most fashionable as guard dogs. Louis XIV had one as a watchdog at the Louvre, and every castle in France had its own. The French revolution brought an end to their popularity and they disappeared from France.

12 **Shar-pei** Shar-peis were originally bred as fighting dogs. They developed their massive, wrinkly skin with harsh bristles as a form of protection, making it difficult for their opponents to get a good grip.

TEN ODD DOGS

1 **Puffinhound** Once well-known in Iceland, the Hebrides and the Orkneys, these days the Puffinhound is only found in Norway. It's the only dog to have a fully-developed fifth toe and it also has the ability to close its ears, thus protecting the inner ear from damage.

2 **Basenji** One of the few native African breeds, the basenji doesn't bark, but it does yodel and whine.

3 **Chow** The chow has a blue-black tongue.

4 **Weimaraner** The Weimaraner comes in a variety of unique shades of grey, from silver to elephant.

5 **Rhodesian ridgeback** The Rhodesian ridgeback has a very obvious ridge of hair along its spine, created by a line of hair growing in the opposite direction to its coat.

6 **Pharaoh hounds** These dogs blush when they get excited – their ears go pink.

7 **Pyrenean mountain dog** This dog has a double dew claw.

8 **Newfoundland** The water-loving Newfoundland has webbed feet.

9 **Shar-pei** Possibly the ugliest of all dogs, the shar-pei's skin is several sizes too large and hangs in big wrinkles all over its body.

10 **Otterhound** The smelliest of the breeds. It spends a great deal of its time in water and has developed a very oily, and very smelly, waterproof coat.

TWO OF THE SHAGGIEST DOGS

There are lots of hairy dogs in the world, but in the history of the shaggy dog the komondor and the puli stand alone. They're not simply shaggy; their coats hang in thick, matted cords like dreadlocks. They're like walking rugs, with only their noses and tongues to be seen. Both are ancient breeds, believed to have come to Hungary from Asia more than a thousand years ago with the Magyars, and despite their looks they're both extremely hard-working and useful dogs.

The komondor, which stands about two feet high, is white and looks very much like the sheep which it is used to herd. The puli is several inches smaller and comes in a variety of colours, and it, too, was used for guarding sheep, for hunting and retrieving in water.

Both are popular as pets and working dogs in Hungary although they're rare in Britain; but if you do ever see a woolly hearthrug walking down a street, you'll know what it is – a komondor or a puli.

THE PRACTICAL POODLE

The poodle is often considered to be one of the dumb blondes of the dog world – an unjust image created by its traditional trim which gives it a prissy, frothy appearance. In fact poodles are one of the most intelligent of all breeds (they were considered for training in war work because of their exceptional brains, but unfortunately they're also very short-sighted!) and were originally used as hunting dogs, retrieving ducks that had been shot down. Because its luxuriant coat got too heavy in water the poodle's hind and fore legs and torso were shaved. Tufts of hair were left around the joints to give the dogs some protection from scrapes and the cold water. In fact the only decorative part of the clip is the bobble on the end of the poodle's tail. So don't laugh when you next see a beautifully-clipped poodle – it's only being practical!

There are a number of accepted poodle clips, but the most common are the lamb clip, the Kerry clip, the English saddle or lion clip, the Continental clip, the Dutch clip and the terrier clip. And if you don't like any of them, why not leave your poodle with its natural shaggy coat?

Lamb clip

Kerry clip

English saddle
(or lion)

Continental clip

Dutch clip

Terrier clip

SIX BREEDS NAMED AFTER THEIR FOUNDERS

Duke of Gordon – Gordon setter According to tradition the Duke returned from a shoot displeased with his own setters' performance. A shepherd lent him a black and brown sheep dog which proved to be so good that he bought her and mated her with one of his setters. It's more likely that the Gordon setter is in fact descended from the spaniel.

Louis Dobermann – Dobermann One of the few dogs that was specially created. Louis Dobermann started the breed in 1870, and although his 'recipe' isn't known it probably included shepherd dogs and cattle dogs. Manchester terrier and greyhound were added at the beginning of this century.

Monsieur Dupuy – Braque Dupuy A French breed created by Monsieur Dupuy to assist him in his work as a game-keeper.

Count A.P. Hamilton – Hamilton Hound or Hamilton-stovare The most popular retriever in Sweden was bred by A.P. Hamilton from German retrievers. It is very rare in Britain.

Bernard of Menthen – the saint who gave his name to the St Bernards that were bred and trained at his hospice in the Alps.

Reverend John Russell – the Jack Russell terrier Many people believe that the Jack Russell is a pedigree dog, but because of the number of variations in colour, size and form it isn't recognised by the Kennel Club.

AND ONE WHICH WASN'T

In the novel *Guy Mannering* Sir Walter Scott created a character called Dandie Dinmont who owned six terriers called Auld Mustard, Young Mustard and Little Mustard and Auld Pepper, Young Pepper and Little Pepper. The character was based on Mr James Davidson who lived in the area and bred terriers whom he called Mustard or Pepper, according to their colour. The breed became recognised in its own right and was christened the Dandie Dinmont terrier in honour of Scott's character.

FIVE THINGS YOU DIDN'T KNOW ABOUT THE PEKINGESE

In the poem 'The More I See Of Men . . .' E.V. Lucas wrote:

The dog will come when he is called,
The cat will turn away;
The Pekingese will please itself
Whatever you may say.

Perhaps the Pekingese's independent spirit has something to do with its extraordinary history. For thousands of years the only people who could own Pekingese dogs were the Emperor of China and a small circle of his courtiers. The dogs were kept in the confines of the Imperial Palace, and it was only when the palace was looted in 1860 that the breed reached Europe. Here are five things you didn't know about the ancient Pekingese.

1 Anyone caught removing a Pekingese from the Imperial Palace was stoned to death. The punishment was carried out as late as this century and the law was only repealed in 1905.
2 The most prized Pekingese were known as sleeve-dogs because they were small enough to be carried in the sleeve of a robe.

3 When an Imperial Pekingese had puppies she didn't look after them herself. They were suckled by human wet nurses, just like the Emperor's own offspring.

4 According to legend the Pekingese got its name 'lion-dog' because the Chinese knew that lions were the fiercest animals on earth. However, because there are no lions in China they weren't sure what one looked like though they knew it had a tuff of hair at the end of its tail. Then one day a sycophantic courtier announced that lions looked just like the fierce little Pekingese that were the favourites of the emperor. They shaved the dogs' tails to make them more lion-like and the lion-dog was born.

5 The first Pekingese to be brought to the west was called Lootie. She was found after the Summer Palace in Peking was sacked in 1860 and rescued by a young English captain called John Hart Dunne. He brought her back as a gift for Queen Victoria, who was famed for her love of dogs, and Lootie was kept at the royal Windsor kennels. She lived there for eleven years and had her portrait painted by Landseer, but the records show that Queen Victoria never visited or saw her Imperial pet.

GIVE A DOG A NAME . . .

Affenpinscher The affenpinscher has a monkey-like face, hence its name. In German *Affe* means monkey and *Pinscher* means terrier.

Basenji The basenji's name comes from the Bantu meaning 'bushman'.

Basset hound The basset originally came from France, where *bas* means low.

Borzoi The name borzoi derives from the Russian phrase *borzaja sobaka*, meaning 'a dog as fast as the wind'.

Cairn When this beed was first established it was given the name short-haired Skye terrier, which fans of the Skye terrier disputed. It was then called a West Highland terrier (it originated in Inverness), which caused protests from West Highland White terrier breeders. Finally, because it was so adept at squeezing into the piles of stones, called cairns, in which its prey hid, it was called the cairn terrier.

Chow In China, where the chow (or chow chow) comes from, *chow* means food, reflecting the fact that the Chinese enjoy eating dog flesh.

Cocker Cocker spaniels got their name because they were originally used as bird dogs and were particularly good at flushing out woodcock.

Corgi From the Welsh *corr* meaning dwarf and *ci* meaning dog, and reflecting the fact that the corgi is a dwarf mutation.

Dachshund From the German *Dachs* meaning badger and *Hund* meaning dog.

Harrier Harriers were used to hunt hares, hence their name.

Keeshond The keeshond is the national breed of Holland. It takes its name from the very common Dutch name of 'Jan Kees' (a sort of Dutch John Smith). When the Dutch went to America they were known collectively as Jan Kees – which in time became 'Yankees'.

Kuvasz A native of Hungary, the kuvasz sheep dog's name is derived from the Turkish word *kawazs* meaning 'the guard of the nobleman'.

Lhasa apso The first part of this breed's name comes from the Tibetan capital, Lhasa. Apso is derived from the Tibetan name for the dog, *abso seng kye* meaning 'barking sentinel dog.'

Mastiff The mastiff is one of the oldest dogs on record. It was first kept as a watch dog or guard dog because of its size, and it's likely that the name comes from the Latin *massivus*, meaning massive.

Papillon The papillon has large butterfly-like ears, and *papillon* is French for butterfly. The phalène, which is from the same breed, has ears that drop back like the wings of a moth and, appropriately, *phalène* is French for moth.

Pug In archaic English 'pug' is a word used to describe ugly, mischievous creatures like elves or goblins, so it could be a reference to the pug's ugly face. Perhaps more likely is the theory that the name is taken from the Latin *pugnus*, meaning fist, which describes the unusual shape of the pug's head.

Saluki The Saluki is known in Persian as *tazi*, meaning Arabian. It is likely that its westernized name is after the vanished Arabian town of Saluk.

Samoyed This breed is named after the Samoyed people of north America, who first domesticated and bred it.

Schipperke This Belgian breed was used on canal barges to keep guard and catch rats. Its name means 'little captain'.

Shih-tzu From the Chinese for 'lion-dog'.

THE HAIR OF THE DOG . . .

As everyone who's ever had a drink too many knows, taking a hair of the dog that bit you is a tried and trusted remedy for dealing with a hangover the next morning. There are at least two explanations for this curious phrase.

The first can be traced back to Roman times, when drinkers used to swallow singed dogs' hair after a night out. Perhaps it worked on the principle that the dog hair tasted so foul the hangover seemed quite bearable! Far tastier is a Hair of the Dog cocktail, which is supposed to be a good pick-me-up if you're suffering from that morning-after feeling. You'll need:

1 oz of Scotch.
1¼ oz of double cream.
½ oz of honey.
Shake all the ingredients with some crushed ice and drain the mixture into a glass. Delicious.

On a different note altogether, the second explanation of the phrase stems from the fear of catching rabies from a dogbite. In the past if a dog bit someone – even a healthy dog – it was killed, for it was feared that if the dog ever became mad, the victim would go mad too. There was another precaution that a victim of dogbite would take. He had to cut some hair from the dog, fry it and then place it on the wound with a sprig of rosemary. Like the original hangover cure, it's not recommended!

DOG SAYINGS

It's amazing how many of our common sayings include references to dogs, though as the dog has been man's companion for thousands of years perhaps we shouldn't be too surprised. Here are just a few doggy proverbs which go to prove how deeply the dog is ingrained in our lives and our language.

Barking dogs seldom bite.
His bark is worse than his bite.
Don't go barking up the wrong tree.
Brag's a good dog but Holdfast goes better which, roughly translated, means that talking is one thing but doing is better.
Dog eat dog, a description of the competitive side of life.
Done up like a dog's dinner.
Every dog has his day, possibly from the time turnspits worked one day on, one day off (see page 121).
Give a dog a bad name and hang him.
Let sleeping dogs lie.
Love me, love my dog.
It's raining cats and dogs.
I wouldn't put a dog out on a night like this.
You can't teach an old dog new tricks.
Going to the dogs.
A black dog sitting on your shoulder (see page 127).
A hair of the dog that bit you.
Give a dog a bone and he can't bite you.
It's no good barking at the moon.
    And finally:
It's a dog's life – and you can interpret that whichever way you choose!

DOG DICTIONARY

Dogs have made a great contribution to the English language but, sadly, the word 'dog' is almost always used to describe something bad. We need some new words to redress the balance! 'Dog' comes from the old English *docga*. It originally seems to have applied to a particular breed of animal rather than the canine race as a whole.

Dog-ape, a dog-faced baboon.

Dog-belt, a coalminer's belt, used for pulling sleds.

Dogberry, a useless constable, bound by bureaucracy, in *Much Ado About Nothing*; now used to describe any petty official.

Dogbolt, a blunt-headed arrow; a term of contempt.

Dog-buffer, a man who stole dogs for their skins.

Dog-bramble, common name for a number of thorny shrubs.

Dog-briar, a wild briar.

Dog-cart, a cart either drawn by dogs, or for carrying sporting dogs, or a simple horse-drawn cart with seats placed back to back.

Dog-cheap, so cheap as to be worthless.

Dog-daisy, the common daisy.

Dog days, hot summer days when the canine star Sirius is in ascent.

Dog-eared, (a book) with the corners of pages turned down; well-used, shabby.

Dog-end, a cigarette stub.

Dog-faced, looking like a dog; used as an insult.

Dog-fall, a wrestling term.

Dog-fennel, common name for *Anthemis cotula*, stinking camomile.

Dogfight, a quick, confused fight.

Dogfish, a small shark; also used to refer to other fishes.

Dog-fox, a male fox.

Dogged, like a dog; cruel, surly, sullen, obstinate.

Dogger, a two-masted fishing boat; a kind of sandy ironstone; an abbreviation for the Dogger Bank, a shoal in the North Sea.

Doggerel, bad verse.

Doggery, bad behaviour; bad language.

Doggo, from the phrase 'to lie doggo', meaning hidden or silent.

Doggone, from the phrase 'dog on it' used by Americans, who often substituted 'dog' for 'god'. May also be a corruption of 'God damn'.

Dog-grass, common name for couch grass.

Doggy, like a dog; a pet name for a little dog; the below-ground manager of a coalmine.

Dog-grate, a detached firegrate sitting in a fireplace and resting on metal supports known as fire-dogs.

Dog-hole, a filthy dwelling; a place fit only for a dog.

Dog house, a kennel.

Dog-hutch, a kennel.

Dog-in-a-blanket, a rolled currant dumpling or jam pudding.

Dog-in-the-manger, a churlish person who won't use something himself (or herself) but won't let anyone else use it either.

Dog-Latin, bad Latin.

Dog-leech, a vet who treats dogs.

Dog-legged, bent like a dog's hind leg; used to describe staircase or golf fairway, for example.

Dog-letter, the letter R.

Dog-nail, a nail with a large countersunk head; large nail with head projecting on one side.

Dog-rose, species of wild rose, *Rosa canina*.

Dog's bane, name given to plants reputed to poison dogs.

Dogsbody, nautical slang for pease pudding; a general drudge.

Dog-sick, completely sick.

Dog-skin, the skin of a dog or leather made from it.

Dog's lady, one way of calling a woman a bitch.

Dog-sleep, light sleep; pretended sleep.

Dog's-meat, food fit only for dogs.

Dog's tail, a genus of grasses in which the flowers all point one way in a shape like a dog's tail.

Dog star, the star Sirius.

Dogstone, a stone used as a millstone.

Dogstones, a name for a number of species of British orchid.

Dog's-tongue, a genus of plants, including hound's-tongue.

Dog's-tooth, a genus of sand-binding grass; a kind of check used in woven tweed fabric.

Dog-tent, a tiny tent, so small it's like a kennel.

Dog-tired, exhausted.

Dog-tree, the common dogwood.

Dog-trick, a mean, low-down trick.

Dog-trot, an easy, relaxed trotting gait.

Dog-watch, the two short watches, 4–6 pm and 6–8 pm, on board ship.

R – THE DOG LETTER

Since Roman times the letter R has been known as the 'dog's letter' or the 'snarling letter' because when pronounced it echoes the growling sound of an angry dog. In many parts of the British Isles, particularly Scotland, the *r* is still pronounced today as a long, rolling *rrrrr*, although in the southeast it has long since become a smooth *r*.

TWELVE TOTALLY TRIVIAL CANINE FACTS

1 The St Bernard rescue dogs did not carry a red cask of brandy around their necks. This was an invention of Sir Edwin Landseer, who included them in a painting entitled 'Alpine Mastiffs Reanimating a Traveller'.
2 The Great Dane doesn't come from Denmark, but from Germany.
3 Champion Akitas are declared national art treasures by the Japanese government.

4 Of all the books in the Bible, only the Book of Tobit in the Apocrypha contains a polite reference to a dog – the others are all anti-dog.

5 The National Greyhound Association keeps a record of noseprints for identifying dogs and preventing fraud.

6 The Mexican hairless dog was bred by Mexican Indians for its meat.

7 The Chihuahua was bred by the Mayans and Toltecs for ritual sacrifice.

8 The whippet was developed by miners in the north of England who wanted racing dogs but couldn't afford to keep a greyhound.

9 To celebrate his conquest of Everest Sherpa Tenzing was given two Lhasa apsos, dogs believed to ward off evil spirits. He became so fond of them that he started breeding them.

10 Louis XIV banned dogs from Versailles and Henry VII banned them from his court.

11 Geoffrey Chaucer was the first person to mention a spaniel in English literature, in *The Wife of Bath's Prologue* in *The Canterbury Tales*.

12 The first successful prosecution for cruelty to dogs occurred in 1835.

DOGS'
TALES

THE ORIGINS OF THE DOG

The origins of the dog go back a long way – forty million years to be precise, when a small carnivorous mammal called *Miacis* flourished and began to evolve into a number of different types of creature. One of the animal 'families' that resulted was the Canidae group, or the dog family. Other of the offshoots were eventually – forty million years allowed plenty of room for development! – to become the cat family, the bear family, the walrus family and even the weasel family!

The dog family is a big one and includes wolves, foxes, jackals, hyenas and coyotes. All members of the family share similar characteristics. They are all carnivorous, they have the same number of toes in the same alignment, they prefer to live in packs and, the fact that clinches the argument, they can be cross-mated. It's possible to cross a dog with a fox, or a dog with a wolf or jackal, and the resulting offspring are healthy and can themselves breed.

There are many different theories about how, from all these animals, the domestic dog developed, but the most widely accepted is that the dog as we know it today is descended from the wolf and the jackal, developing and interbreeding differently throughout the world to give us the wide variety of breeds we take for granted. The only exception to this is the dingo, which is the one true purebred wild dog in the world.

The next great mystery in the story of the dog is the question – how did it become domesticated? No one knows. Perhaps, fourteen thousand years ago, hunters killed dogs for food, found puppies and kept them. Then maybe they realised that with their superior senses of hearing and smell the dogs would make good guard and hunting animals. It's possible that the dog initiated the relationship, hanging around the homes of early man in the hope of picking up scraps and bones and eventually becoming an accepted part of life. Who knows? All that can be said for certain is that at

Starr Carr Stone Age settlement in Yorkshire remains of a dog were discovered among all the other evidence of life and dated at around 7500 BC. By 4000 BC Egyptian artists were portraying hounds on the tomb wall of Senbi, Prince of Cusae, and by the first century AD dogs were regularly featuring in the art and ceramics of China, Greece, Assyria and Italy, proving that they had established themselves as a popular feature of human civilisation.

EIGHT MYTHICAL DOGS

Actaeon's hounds Actaeon was a great hunter and had a pack of fifty of the fastest and most wonderful hounds. One day when he was out hunting he had the misfortune to come across the goddess of chastity, Artemis, bathing in a pool. She turned him into a stag for his impudence and he was chased and torn to pieces by his own hounds.

Anubis was the jackal-god of ancient Egypt. He helped Osiris in his task of judging the dead by weighing their hearts against the feathers of light and truth. When Osiris was cut into many pieces by Set, Anubis helped collect all the parts together and assemble them again as the first mummy. He is particularly associated with death, embalming and the guarding of tombs.

Bran was a legendary dog mentioned in both Irish and Scottish legend. In the Irish story he belonged to Finn MacCool; in Scottish tales he is Fingal's dog. In both legends he was an immensely strong dog, which was why to keep him chained up they had to attach him to a rock formation near Dunolly Castle – rocks which are still known as Bran's Pillars.

Cerberus was the three-headed dog that guarded the entrance to Hades. It had a serpent's tail and a mane of serpents too – certainly not a Kennel Club approved breed. One of the labours of Hercules was to drag this monster into the upper world, and this he did. When the Greeks buried a corpse they included with the body a piece of honey-soaked cake with which to appease the guardian of the underworld. This has given us the saying 'a sop to Cerberus'.

Lelaps In Greek mythology Lelaps was an infallible hound, owned by the nymph Procris, which was guaranteed to catch whatever it chased. One day Lelaps saw a hare and began to chase it, little knowing that the hare had been destined never to be caught. Rather than having a never-ending chase Zeus turned both Lelaps and the hare to stone.

Maera was a faithful dog who belonged to Icarius. When his master was killed by shepherds and his body flung down a well Maera led his daughter Erigone to his body. She was so overcome that she killed herself and Maera flung himself down the well. All three were placed among the stars. Icarius became the constellation Boötes, Erigone became Virgo and Maera became Canicula.

The Mauthe Dog is a spectral hound that is said to haunt Peel Castle on the Isle of Man. It's a ghostly black spaniel that has been seen for generations in the guard room there; when it made its appearance the guards were careful to behave themselves, because people found drunk and disorderly by the Mauthe Dog tended to come to a sticky end . . .

Orthros was the two-headed dog that guarded the red cattle of the monster Geryon. Hercules' tenth labour was to slay Orthros and make off with the cattle.

114

THE DOG OF MONTARGIS

In 1371 during the reign of King Charles VI of France, a nobleman called Aubri de Mondidier was murdered, while out hunting in the Forest of Bondi, by his companion Macaire, who buried the body and made his escape. Mondidier's dog, an Irish wolfhound, was not present at the time of the attack but he found his master's grave and lay down on it. When hunger and thirst grew too much to bear, the dog went back to Paris and howled and scratched at the door of one of his master's friends. When the man answered the dog took him by the sleeve and guided him back through the forest to the spot where Mondidier's grave could be seen. The friend inspected the grave, found his friend's body and adopted the faithful hound as his own.

But the story didn't end there. The dog's new master took him to court and there the dog recognised Macaire and sprang at him. It took several people to drag him away, and all were bemused by this unusual behaviour. Irish wolfhounds didn't normally attack unless provoked, they knew, and they also remembered that before his death Mondidier had been involved in an argument with Macaire. To test their suspicions the King ordered both Macaire and the dog to be brought before him, and again the dog went for the man. The king decided that the evidence against Macaire was so strong that he should stand trial, and because the dog couldn't appear as a witness in a court of law, the trial would be by ordeal of battle. Throughout the Middle Ages all kinds of difficult disputes were solved in this way because it was believed that the innocent would always triumph over the guilty.

A fight to the death between a man and an animal was something new and dense crowds turned up to watch when the combat was held on the Isle de la Cité. Macaire was armed with a long club and the dog was given a barrel to retreat into when it needed to get its breath back. The fight went on for a long time and Macaire managed to hold the dog off, but at last he became exhausted with the effort of swinging the heavy club and gave the animal an opportunity to leap up and grab him by the throat. Just as it pushed him to the ground and was about to finish him off, Macaire shouted out and admitted his guilt, and the dog immediately freed him and stood back so that he could be taken away and hanged. A mural depicting this duel was painted in Charles VI's castle at Montargis, which is how the dog got its name.

STAGE DOGS

The legend of the dog of Montargis might have been forgotten if there hadn't been a fashion in the early nineteenth century for dramas written specifically for dogs to perform. Charles-Guilbert de Pixerécourt knew a good dog story when he heard one and promptly wrote a play entitled *The Dog of Montargis, The Forest of Bondi*, which was a sensation in Paris. So successful was it that it was translated into seven languages and played in England for 1,100 performances. It wasn't the human actors that the audience packed in to see but the canine performers, who received standing ovations night after night.

When early film-makers came to look for simple subjects to transfer to celluloid they recognised the popularity of stage dog dramas and decided to cash in. This is why so many early movies were about dogs; *Rescued by Rover*, the Strongheart films, Rin Tin Tin and even Lassie all owe a debt to a fourteenth-century legend!

THE STORY OF OLD DRUM

If you're the least bit sentimental about dogs, get the tissues ready now because the story of Old Drum is a sad one. In October 1869 a Missouri farmer's nephew took a shotgun and killed Old Drum, his neighbour's dog, because he believed he was worrying the sheep.

The old dog hadn't been – he was a farm dog born and bred and knew better than that – and so his owner took the case to court. The result of the court case has been forgotten, but what stayed in the memory of everyone who heard it was the summing-up given by George Vest, the lawyer speaking for the prosecution. It took more than an hour, an hour during which Vest explored the relationship between man (and woman) and dog. It seemed to sum up the way many people felt about their dogs, and local people were so moved that they built a monument at the spot where Old Drum had died.

Vest's speech was remembered for many years, and in 1953 a statue, complete with the text, was erected at the courthouse where the trial had been held. There isn't room to reproduce the whole speech, but here's just a sample from it. Do you still have your hankie handy?

The one absolutely unselfish friend that a man can have in this world is his dog . . . If fortune drives the master forth an outcast in the world, . . . the faithful dog asks no higher privilege than that of accompanying him . . . and when the last scene of all comes, and death takes his master in its embrace . . . there by the graveside will the noble dog be found, his head between his paws, his eyes sad but open in alert watchfulness, faithful and true even to death.

THE FIRST TAIL-DOCKING?

Tail-docking is an emotive subject. For many years dozens of breeds have routinely had their tails docked a few days after birth, usually by having the end of the tail cut off with special clippers. All sorts of familiar dogs are docked routinely – boxers, Dobermanns, spaniels, bulldogs and many terriers among them – but an increasing number of people feel that it is a cruel and unnecessary practice. Originally docking was carried out so that hunting dogs didn't get themselves caught in undergrowth when following their quarry, a reason which seems rather senseless these days when most dogs are kept as pets.

One person who docked his dogs and got into trouble for doing so was Alcibiades who, according to the Greek writer Plutarch, owned a wonderful dog with a very luxuriant tail. Alcibiades was a playboy and lived a thoroughly immoral life; so much so that the good folk of Athens threw him out of the city. When he was called back in 407 BC he brought with him his dog, and immediately had its tail docked. There was public outrage at the act, which was just what Alcibiades wanted. While everyone was furious with him for docking the poor dog they forgot about his bad reputation!

KING DOG!

If legend is correct, Norway must be one of the only countries in the world to have been ruled by a dog. Many years ago – sometime around 1001–23 if historical records can be relied on – King Eystein of Norway was driven out of the country by his people, who didn't like the way he was running things. The exiled king gathered an army, marched back and won the battle to regain his throne. Then he decided to impose a punishment on his people. If they didn't like him as king, he told them, they could have a choice of monarch – a choice between a slave and a dog.

The Norwegian people decided that a dog would be less trouble than a man and King Saur I was crowned. There is no information on the kind of breed the new king was, but he was called Majesty by all and lived a royal life, being carried around when it was cold and wet so that he wouldn't get his feet damp. He reigned for three years, signing laws with his paw and passing judgement with his barks, and everyone obeyed his orders.

Then one day tragedy struck. The dog king was out in a meadow enjoying himself when a wolf pounced on a lamb nearby. The brave king promptly pounced on the wolf, and before his astonished subjects could come to his rescue, was killed. He was given a state funeral and it was decided that perhaps a human successor would be a better idea than another dog.

THE BEAUTIFUL BOXER

If you've always thought of boxers, with their squashed-up faces, as charming but ugly, you may be surprised to know that according to legend the boxer is the most beautiful dog of all. The story goes that the boxer was the last dog created by God, who fashioned it lovingly out of clay before declaring it to be absolutely perfect. The dog was so excited that it couldn't wait until the clay dried to take a look at itself. It ran headlong towards the nearest mirror – and squashed its perfect face against the glass. So next time you see a boxer, remember, it's not ugly, it's beautiful!

THE TURNSPIT

For many centuries no great kitchen could run smoothly without the aid of a turnspit, a small, long-backed, short-legged dog who was employed to turn a spit on which joints of meat were cooked. Before dogs were used small boys did this sweaty, unpleasant task and got under the feet of the cook, whose job it was to baste the joint with hot fat. Then during the Middle Ages someone had the idea of building a dog-sized treadmill and training a dog to run round in it, turning the spit as it went.

It was hard work. A large joint of beef could take several hours to cook, during which time it had to be constantly rotated. In some great houses a pair of turnspits were kept so that they could work on alternate days without becoming too exhausted. The dogs knew their days and refused to work when their companion was supposed to be in the wheel. In fact it's likely that the saying 'Every dog has his day' has its origins in this shared work of the turnspits.

Turnspits were cruelly mistreated if they stopped treading the wheel. Hot coals were placed at their feet to keep them moving, so it was no wonder that they rarely came willingly to work, as a seventeenth-century poet observed:

'. . . The dinner must be dished at once,
Where's this vexatious turnspit gone?
Unless the skulking cur is caught,
The sirloin's spoilt, and I'm in fault.'
Thus said (for sure you'll think it fit
That I the cook maid's oaths omit),
With all the fury of a cook,
Her coller kitchen Nan forsook:
The broomstick o'er her head she waves,
She sweats, she stamps, she puffs, she raves –
The sneaking cur before her flies;
She whistles, calls, fair speech she tries;
These nought avail. Her choler burns;
The fist and cudgel threat by turns.
With hasty stride she presses near:
He slinks aloof, and howls with fear.

Not all of the cooks can have been cruel, however, for some of them used to take their turnspit dogs with them to church – or perhaps they only used them to sit on their feet and keep them warm through the sermon, which was the reason so many nuns took their small lapdogs, known as 'comforters', to services. On one particular fifteenth-century

Sunday the Bishop of Gloucester was giving the lesson in the Abbey church in Bath. He took as his text the first chapter of Ezekiel, which makes great use of the word 'wheel' – '. . . and the wheels were lifted up over against them: for the spirit of the living creature was in the wheels . . .' and so on. The poor turnspits, hearing this familiar and hated word, raced out of the church with their tails between their legs and jumped straight into their own wheels!

In the eighteenth century the turnspit was made redundant when a new-fangled clockwork roasting spit was introduced, and it was only in the most rural areas that the dogs were kept. The last few were still working in 1870, when it was noted that they had now become so unusual that owners could make 6d a day if they cared to hire them to others, but by the turn of the century the turnspit, as a breed, was extinct.

THE DIABETIC DOG

The first animal to be kept alive with insulin was Marjorie, a black and white mongrel who was kept at the University of Toronto. Her pancreas was removed to make her diabetic and then she was put on a course of insulin, which was the only thing that could save her life. She lived for seventy days after the operation and died in July 1921. Her contribution to science was immeasurable, because it gave doctors the confidence to use insulin on diabetic humans who, until then, had been almost certainly doomed. Six months after the experiment on Marjorie thirteen-year-old Leonard Thompson became the first human to receive this life-saving therapy.

DOGNAPPED!

In 1843 Elizabeth Barrett Browning's cocker spaniel Flush was stolen and held to ransom for £50, becoming perhaps the most famous victim of dognappers on record. Fortunately, after three days of waiting, Flush was returned to his tearful mistress.

Dogs have always been valuable and from the tenth century they were traded. In fact Howell the Good, the King of Wales, set down rules as early as AD 920 for defining the precise value of any dog. Prices ranged from 4d to £1! From this time onwards dog stealing became a common crime. The tactics used by dognappers were sophisticated and they preyed in particular on ladies' dogs, because women were supposed to have softer hearts when it came to paying up for their pets. No dog owner was safe – not even the king. In 1660 when one of his dogs was stolen, Charles II was so desperate he put this advertisement in the *Mercurius Publicus*, one of the newspapers of the day:

> We must call upon you again for a black dog, between a greyhound and a spaniel, no white about him, only a streak on his breast, and his tail a little bobbed. It is his Majesty's own dog, and doubtless was stolen, for the dog was not born or bred in England, and would never forsake his master. Whosoever finds him may acquaint any at Whitehall, for the dog was better known at court than those who stole him: Will they never leave off robbing his Majesty? Must he not keep a dog? This dog's place, though better than some imagine, is the only place which nobody offers to beg.

Maybe it was the memory of this incident that led a later Prince of Wales to provide his Great Dane (which had been a present from the poet Alexander Pope, whose own Great Dane, Bounce, was much admired) with a collar on which was written the rhyme:

I am his Highness' dog at Kew.
Pray tell me, sir, whose dog are you?

THE DAISY DOG

According to legend, in the sixteenth century the Emperor of China decided to honour Elizabeth I of England by sending her a pair of his Pekingese dogs. To accompany the dogs on their journey one of the royal princesses was chosen as an escort, and she set off with her charges in a carved ivory box. On the long journey to England the Pekingese bitch gave birth to a litter of five puppies. The party reached France safely and found a Cornish boat to take them on the last leg of the voyage across the Channel, but once on board the crew became suspicious of the princess and her exotic looks. She was, they said, a demon, and her carved ivory box contained treasure. Their opinion was hardened when, just off the Cornish coast, a storm blew up. Terrified, the sailors broke into the princess's cabin and one man picked up the box. The little dog, guarding his family inside, bit the sailor through the ivory bars and the man dropped the animals overboard. The princess was also thrown into the sea. Immediately the wind dropped and the ship sailed safely away.

The princess's body and the box containing the dogs were washed on to the shore at a deserted cove near Land's End. None of the locals would go near it, fearing the Chinese devil, but one man, the village simpleton, dared to approach. He found that only one of the dogs, the fierce little father, was alive, and he was dying. While everyone else stood back, the simpleton dug a grave and placed the princess and the bitch and puppies in it. Then he planted a cross of wild daisies on top and settled the Pekingese among them. The dog licked his hand and died.

Meanwhile, the ship reached shore safely and the sailors told the story of the demon they'd thrown overboard. Not long afterwards the man who'd been bitten died, and once more everyone shunned the spot where the princess was buried. It was said that the ghost of the little Daisy dog still haunted the grave, guarding his puppies and mistress, and one bite from him was enough to kill. Maybe he is still guarding them, for in 1850 it was reported that a boy found a piece of carved ivory near the cliffs of the bay. When he picked it up he felt as if he had been bitten, and he died. Perhaps he too had been bitten by the Daisy dog.

BLACK SHUCK

If you're ever walking down a dark lane in East Anglia late at night and you hear the pad of doggy feet at your side, turn away! It could be Black Shuck, the demon dog which is said to haunt large areas of Suffolk, Norfolk and Cambridgeshire, and a glimpse of him means death. In fact he could be one of a number of Black Shucks in East Anglia, all of them different. 'Shuck' is taken from the Anglo-Saxon word *scucca*, which means demon; it's likely that the legends of a black demon dog go back many hundreds of years.

At Clopton Hall, Suffolk, Black Shuck is said to appear with the body of a monk and the head of a dog as he guards a hoard of gold. In Norfolk he takes the shape of one of the wolves who inhabited the area during the Middle Ages, and howls during storms. Motorists have swerved across roads to avoid the demon and pedestrians have reported feeling Black Shuck's breath on their necks as they walked home – though it's not recorded whether they were on their way home from the pub at the time!

If you're on a lonely road in Essex, however, and a fearsome black dog appears, there's no need to panic. The Essex Shuck, unlike his local counterparts, is a friendly creature who likes to escort lonely travellers on their journeys.

The threat of bad luck that was said to accompany a sighting of Black Shuck, and other ghostly black dogs found throughout Britain, may explain the origin of the saying 'a black dog is sitting on his shoulder' to describe someone in a state of depression.

IT'S A DOG'S LIFE

THE TOP TWENTY BREEDS OF 1986

The Kennel Club compiles a list of the twenty most popular breeds registered each year. In 1986 these were:

1	German shepherd (Alsatian)	19,309
2	Retriever (Labrador)	14,625
3	Retriever (golden)	11,948
4	Yorkshire terrier	10,637
5	Cavalier King Charles spaniel	9,766
6	Dobermann	8,564
7	Rottweiler	8,374
8	Spaniel (cocker)	7,121
9	Spaniel (English springer)	6,474
10	Staffordshire bull terrier	6,473
11	Boxer	5,185
12	West Highland white terrier	5,155
13	Collie (rough)	4,479
14	Shetland sheepdog	3,146
15	Cairn terrier	2,322
16	Bull terrier	2,263
17	Poodle (toy)	2,166
18	Great Dane	2,068
19	Irish setter	1,790
20	Pekingese	1,727

FIVE DOGS GOING OUT OF FASHION

		1979	1986
1	Afghan hound	2,098	665
2	Dachshund (smooth-haired)	712	333
3	Irish setter	5,190	1,790
4	Old English sheepdog	5,731	1,725
5	Yorkshire terrier	19,187	10,637

FIVE DOGS COMING INTO FASHION

		1979	1986
1	Akita	2	296
2	Bouvier des Flandres	30	136
3	Rottweiler	1,033	8,374
4	Shar-pei	0	124
5	Staffordshire bull terrier	2,792	6,473

FIVE BOTTOM KENNEL CLUB BREEDS

The Kennel Club's 'league table' of the most popular pedigree dogs in the country shows a number of breeds that had no registrations at all in 1986. Many of these were newly recognised breeds, but others were breeds that are rarely found as pedigree pets in this country.

1 American water spaniel: 12 registered in 1981, none since then.
2 Australian kelpie: 5 registered in 1981, none since then.
3 Small Münsterländer: 1 in 1981, none since then.
4 Fox hound: 3 registered in 1985, none since.
5 Hungarian kuvasz: 1 registered in 1979, none since then.

DOGS BY NUMBERS

DOG POPULATION

* There were estimated to be 6.3 million dogs in 5.1 million households in Britain in 1986. Dogs are the most popular household pets, with cats a very close second.

* Of households which own a dog, 82% own one dog and 18% have two or more.
* Dogs are most popular in homes which are detached, semi-detached or terraced, notably in rural areas.
* Dog ownership is highest in the Midlands and the North.
* The age group in which the percentage of dog owners is highest is 35–54. In contrast to this, cats tend to appeal to a lower age group, 35–45, and are most common in the South, Wales and East Anglia.
* In terms of socio-economic groups, dog owners are found at all levels of society. There are 21.3 million households in this country and out of them 5.1 million own dogs. The households split up like this:

SOCIAL GROUP % HOUSEHOLDS OWNING DOGS

AB	14%
C1	23%
C2	28%
DE	33%

* The most popular breeds of dogs are Alsatians, Labradors, Yorkshire terriers and Jack Russells.
* The total number of dogs registered with the Kennel Club in 1986 was 189,416.
* There are probably between 120 and 150 million dogs worldwide; 35 million live in the USA alone.

DOGS' DINNERS

Before the 1930s most dogs lived on the scraps from their owners' tables. Then someone invented tinned dog food – and look what happened . . .

* In 1986 dog owners spent £407 million on prepared food for their pets. They also spent £35,922,000 on 484,000 tonnes of dog 'treats', including biscuits and chocolate drops.
* 90% of dog owners use prepared foods of one sort or another – canned, moist, dog meal, biscuits or treats – and British dogs eat more tinned food per head than dogs anywhere else in the world.
* The biggest petfood manufacturer in this country is Pedigree Petfoods; Spillers are the second largest. Pedigree Petfoods has the biggest canning factory – of any kind – in Europe.
* According to Spillers the liver, rabbit and turkey varieties of tinned dog food are the most popular.
* *Chappie* was the first brand of tinned dog food sold in Britain, and it's still being sold today.
* During the war tinned dog food was not available because there was no tinplate for the cans. Instead, British dog owners bought dogfood in glass jars!

* Pedigree *Chum* is the best-selling brand of tinned dogfood in the UK. Their adverts, which each year boast that the latest Cruft's Supreme Champion has been fed on *Chum*, are true. Throughout the 1970s and 80s only two Supreme Champions have been fed on another brand.

* The principal ingredients of petfood are meat and meat by-products, including offal and parts of carcases that custom and usage dictate are unsuitable for human consumption. In many ways petfood manufacturers use material that would otherwise be thrown away or wasted. Fish and cereals are also used and maize is now being increasingly introduced.

* Members of the Pet Food Manufacturers' Association – which includes all the major manufacturers in the UK – do not use horse, pony, whale or kangaroo meat in their products.

* Although not intended for human consumption, and not to be recommended, no harm has been caused to people who have eaten dog food. One inventor of a well-known brand of tinned dog food ate his product for breakfast to prove that it was acceptable to humans and in 1984 a round-the-world yachtsman who wanted to take the most efficient and lightest form of nutrition on his voyage was advised, after tests on all kinds of dried food, to stock his galley with moist pre-packed dog food. Maybe he didn't fancy it; anyway, he didn't set sail!

* An American food editor called Raymond A. Solokov decided to give the taste test to a number of dog foods on the market. His findings were recorded in *Man Bites Dog Foods and Finds Some to His Liking*. He tried various types of food ranging from raw mince to canned horsemeat chunks and also offered them to a Saluki bitch called Cleo to see if she agreed with his findings. She was far less fussy than he was and ate almost everything, including *Daily All-Breed*, a cheap liver flavour mix, brown-green in colour, which he couldn't bring himself to swallow. Mr Solokov's favourite foods were raw minced beef, which he gave his top rating, and a milk-based dog biscuit which was so tasty that he ate two with the comment, 'Could replace Ry-Krisp'!

DOGS' DO

---

* 1,000,000 kilos of dog faeces and 4,500,000 litres of urine are deposited on pavements in this country each day, according to the National Consumer Council. If your dog prefers to puddle indoors, take a tip from Buckingham Palace. It's reported that wherever the royal corgis go, soda syphons are kept at hand. A good shot of soda water stops puddles staining carpets and neutralises the smell.

GREAT AND SMALL

* The **tallest** breeds of dog are the Great Dane and the Irish wolfhound, both of which can exceed heights of 39 inches.

* The **smallest** breed is the Chinese Imperial ch'in, not a Kennel Club recognised breed, which stands between 3 and 6 inches tall. More usually accepted as the smallest breeds are the Chihuahua and the Pekingese, which stand somewhere between 6 and 9 inches tall.

* According to the *Guinness Book of Records* the **oldest** reliably recorded age for a dog is 29 years and 5 months for an Australian cattle dog.

* The record for the **largest** litter of puppies goes to an American foxhound who had 23. The British record went to an Irish setter who had 22 puppies in 1974.

* The **strongest** dogs are St Bernards and Newfoundlands, both of which can haul heavy loads.

DOG SENSE

So far the dog's senses of taste and touch have defied quantification by scientists, but they have been able to shed some light on the amazing keenness of the dog's other three senses . . .

SIGHT

In daylight, a dog's sight is generally accepted to be weaker than a human's. Although dogs have a wider field of vision than us, they find it difficult to distinguish a still object at a distance of 300 yards. Poodles are known to be particularly short-sighted. Dogs with protruding eyes, like the bulldog and the boxer, seem also to have problems with short-sightedness. At night, however, the situation is reversed and the dog can see much better than its owner. This ability has developed because of the dog's original role as a nocturnal hunter.

Although there is some dispute about the findings, evidence indicates that dogs are almost completely colour blind. They can distinguish between light and dark shades, but they don't see colour as we do. Many dog owners have disputed this and insisted that their dogs can recognise a particular coloured jacket or towel, but in these cases it's likely that the dog recognises the smell of the dye or fabric just as much as the colour. In fact dogs don't seem to see much detail – they tend to recognise things from their basic shape and use their other senses, particularly smell, to help identify them.

SMELL

The dog's sense of smell has been estimated to be one hundred times more acute than man's. What that means in practice is that where we might wake up in the country on a spring morning and think to ourselves that the air smells wonderfully fresh, a dog can identify all the different smells that contribute to the general freshness – blossom, pollen, new-cut grass, the sea and so on. Or put it another way; most dogs can detect a single drop of blood in ten pints of water.

The sense of smell relies on olfactory nerves in the nose and dogs have many more of these nerves than man. The average man has around five million. The figures for dogs are impressive, and the bigger the dog and longer its nose, the better, generally speaking, its sense of smell.

Dachshund	125 million
Fox terrier	147 million
Alsatian	200 million

In many countries this sensitive sniffing equipment is used commercially. In Denmark and Holland, for example, dogs are used to trace gas leaks because they are far more efficient than electronic instruments. They may not, however, be as efficient as pigs. When the United States army wanted to develop an animal for sniffing out mines and explosives they tried a number of species and the pig turned out to be overall champion – not surprising, perhaps, if one considers that it has always been used in France to find truffles. Unfortunately no one in the army could face the idea of being towed around by a sniffer pig and the dog continues its work!

HEARING

The dog's sense of hearing is almost as keen as its sense of smell. Humans can only just hear a noise of 30,000 cycles per second, while dogs have been shown to respond to 100,000. A sound that a human fails to hear at 12ft can be detected by a dog at 75ft. This goes a long way to explaining why dogs seem to be able to 'predict' things like the arrival of a person or a car. It's not that they have some kind of extra sensory perception, just that their extraordinary combination of hearing and smell allow them to detect the approach of someone long before we ever notice it.

CRUFT'S – DOG BISCUITS TO DOG SHOWS

In the canine world February is the most important month of the year; it's then that Cruft's Dog Show, the most famous dog show in Britain, is held. Cruft's was started by Charles Cruft, a man who decided very early in his life that his future prosperity lay in dogs. In 1876 he became a salesman for James Spratt, selling Spratt's 'dog cakes' – the first specially-made product aimed at the dog food market. On a trip to the USA Spratt had noted the way in which a consignment of unwanted ship's biscuits had been marketed as 'dog cakes' and had been snapped up immediately by dog owners. Guessing that British owners would be equally enthusiastic he sailed home, bringing with him some slabs of dried buffalo meat which he cooked up with more ship's biscuits to make Spratt's Dog Cakes. He was right, and soon had a booming business in which Charles Cruft helped, visiting kennels housing sporting dogs and selling them Dog Cakes.

Cruft's work took him to France, too, and it was there in 1878 that he was invited to promote a dog show at the Paris Exhibition. This was a success and from there the idea for Cruft's dog shows developed. In those days it was possible for an individual to organise and run a dog show for personal profit and Cruft, recognising a growing interest in breeding pedigree dogs, booked the Royal Agricultural Hall in Islington in 1891 for his own show. It became an annual event, and a very profitable one for him. Today there are no privately-run dog shows and the Kennel Club only grants show licences to non-profit-making organisations.

After Charles Cruft's death in 1938 his widow organised one more show and there was then a gap until 1948, when the Kennel Club took over, retaining the name. Since then it has gone from strength to strength, with only two years, 1949 and 1954, passing without a Cruft's Dog Show. 1986 saw the 90th Show and in 1987 Cruft's had to be held for four days, instead of the usual three, because of the sheer number of entrants.

TWENTY CRUFT'S TOP DOGS

In 1928 the tradition of choosing a Best in Show dog was introduced. Here are the winners of this ultimate top dog award over the last twenty years.

1968 Fanhill Faune	Lakeland terrier
1969 Hendrawen's Nibelung of Charavigne	Alsatian
1970 Bergerie Knur	Pyrenean mountain dog
1971 Ramacon Swashbuckler	Alsatian
1972 Abraxas Audacity	Bull terrier
1973 Alansmere Aquarius	Cavalier King Charles
1974 Burtonswood Bossy Boots	St Bernard
1975 Brookewire Brandy of Layven	Fox terrier
1976 Dianthus Buttons	West Highland white
1977 Bournehouse Dancing Master	English setter
1978 Harrowhill Huntsman	Wire-haired fox terrier
1979 Callaghan of Leander	Kerry blue terrier

1980 Shargleam Blackcap	Flat-coated retriever
1981 Astley's Portia of Rua	Irish setter
1982 Grayco Hazelnut	Toy poodle
1983 Montravia Kaskarak Hitari	Afghan hound
1984 Saxonsprings Hackensack	Lhasa apso
1985 Montravia Tommy-Gun	Standard poodle
1986 Ginger Xmas Carol	Airedale
1987 Viscount Grant	Afghan hound

MULTIPLE TOP DOGS

From the time that the Best in Show accolade was established in 1928 to 1950, during which period there were fourteen Cruft's Dog Shows, four dogs each won the award twice. Six awards were won by three cocker spaniels, all owned by H.S. Lloyd: Luckystar of Ware (1930 and 1931), Exquisite Model of Ware (1938 and 1939) and Tracey Witch of Ware (1948 and 1950). Lorna Countess Howe's Labrador retriever Bramshaw Bob won it twice in 1932 and 1933. Since then no other cocker spaniel has won the title and only one Labrador retriever, Cheveralla Ben of Banchory, has achieved it (in 1937). He, like the other champion Labrador retriever, was owned by Lorna Countess Howe.

SIX THINGS TO DO IF YOU MEET AN UNFRIENDLY DOG

There are no firm rules about what you should do if you are confronted by an unfriendly dog, but these tips should be useful in averting trouble.

1 Most dogs will bark if you enter their territory – it's their job to guard it. Talk to the dog firmly but quietly and, if its hackles are down and it's not snarling, stand still so that it can sniff you.
2 If a dog backs away or stays put as you approach it probably means that he regards you as dominant and will be too scared to attack. If he stands straight up, snarls, holds his tail high, stares and comes slowly towards you, be on your guard and back slowly away.
3 Don't walk quickly away from a dog, or attempt to race past it. This kind of action may release his chase instinct.
4 Try not to look afraid. Dogs can read fear in your eyes and movements. By keeping calm and speaking firmly you will prove that the dog has no need to be afraid of you.
5 Don't stare at a dog. In dog language a stare is a threat.
6 Always back away from a dog and never turn your back on it. Many dogs wouldn't dare attack you face on but can't resist a nip at your departing back.

(Information courtesy of the RSPCA)

SEVEN BREEDS OF DOG THAT BITE THE LEAST

According to a survey of vets in the London area in 1982, these seven breeds of dog were the least likely to bite.

1 Labrador
2 Golden retriever
3 Boxer
4 Yorkshire terrier
5 Great Dane
6 Irish wolfhound
7 Basset hound

NINE BREEDS THAT BITE THE MOST

Dr Robert Oleson on the US Public Health authority has studied the dogs most likely to bite for more than twenty years. Apparently the month in which you're most likely to be bitten is June – in America at least.

1 Alsatian/German shepherd
2 Chow
3 Poodle
4 Italian bulldog
5 Fox terrier
6 Chow cross
7 Airedale terrier
8 Pekingese
9 Alsatian cross

In Britain you're more likely to be bitten by terriers, particularly Jack Russells, pedigree collies, Dobermanns and highly-strung spaniels, according to vets who believe that over-breeding of some very popular dogs is creating changes in temperament. All vets and experts agree that if you're looking for a good-tempered dog it's hard to beat a mongrel whose hunting and territorial instincts will have been diluted by inter-breeding.

FIVE EXCUSES FOR NOT NEUTERING YOUR DOG – AND REPLIES

Every day in Britain more than 2,000 dogs are destroyed simply because they are unwanted. Thousands more roam the streets causing a nuisance in traffic, fouling pavements and giving all dogs a bad name. Responsible dog owners *know* that they should have their pets neutered but a surprising number make excuses for not doing so and end up with a litter of puppies. Here are some of the excuses they come up with, and some of the facts to which they are turning a blind eye.

1 **It doesn't matter if our dog has puppies. We can always find good homes for them.**
   This may be true, but how many of the puppies are still in those good homes a year or two later? One of the National Canine Defence League's kennels reported that a local

breeder's puppies were regularly being brought in as unwanted pets. Six from a single litter turned up one by one. When the NCDL contacted the breeder to inform her of the problem she insisted that her dogs 'were in great demand'. Maybe they were as tiny puppies, but as larger dogs no one wanted to keep them.

2 **There's always an animal welfare society to take care of them.**
There simply aren't enough good homes for every dog, and no matter how hard the animal welfare societies try to find places for them more than a hundred thousand perfectly healthy dogs (some welfare organisations estimate up to 250,000) who would make excellent pets, are put down each year.

3 **Nature intended animals to breed. It's unnatural to interfere with them.**
Because of the way we feed and care for our pets they are capable of having many more healthy puppies than they would if they were undomesticated. We already interfere in their lives; refusing to neuter them on these grounds is quite unrealistic.

4 **Spaying makes bitches fat – and anway, one litter of puppies helps a bitch to settle down and develop a good character.**
Neither is true. Bitches don't get fat unless they are overfed and pregnancy doesn't change temperament.

5 **It's too expensive to have a pet neutered.**
Vet's fees, food and even time off work to look after a pregnant bitch are far more expensive than having her spayed. Many animal clinics and animal organisations offer reductions for people in difficult financial circumstances. In fact if you care about your pet there's really no excuse at all for not having it neutered.

THE LAW OF THE CHASE

These days we take our right to own a dog very much for granted, but it hasn't always been so. From Anglo-Saxon times until the sixteenth century there were stringent rules about who could, and could not, own certain types of dogs. It started when Canute, who loved hunting, became king. He forbade anyone except 'freemen' (and there weren't many of those around because most of the population were serfs) to own a greyhound. Those who were eligible to own greyhounds had to have their dogs mutilated to stop them chasing the king's deer and game, and among the methods used were cutting off the ball of a greyhound's foot or striking off three of its toes.

Dogs other than greyhounds or mastiffs *were* allowed to roam, unmutilated, in the royal forests that covered most of the country provided that they were small. Dog measures were kept to determine legal sizes. These stirrup-shaped measures were around six inches in diameter, which meant that only lap-dogs were small enough to pass through them. Gradually these laws were relaxed and the measures got bigger, but they were still in use in the 1700s.

For any medieval dog-lover these laws were repressive but owning a dog could be positively dangerous. A dog, however small, had only to run after a deer to bring the owner up in court. And any dog-owner who was suspected of poaching had to be extremely careful; until Richard I's reign the penalty for poaching entailed castration, blinding and having both hands and feet cut off . . .

DOGS BEWARE

From the medieval period and into the eighteenth century, August was a bad month for dogs. During the hot 'dog days' of the summer the officers of every city were under orders to kill as many strays as they could get their hands on. When, during the seventeenth century, it was realised that there was a link between the plague and rats, cats and dogs – it was the plague flea, though no one knew it – things got even worse and dogs were rounded up and massacred in their thousands. The dog-killers who specialised in this work were instantly recognisable; they wore uniforms made from dog skins. When the Great Plague hit London in 1666 40,000 dogs were destroyed by the dog-killers. Cats came off even worse, and an amazing 200,000 met their end.

Wars spell bad news for dogs too. In the first few weeks after World War II broke out 400,000 dogs were put down by owners who remembered the rationing and anti-dog feeling that had made life so difficult during World War I.

CANINE CONSTABLES

Ever since the first parish constables went on their rounds accompanied by their pet dogs in the fifteenth century, there have been unofficial police dogs at work. But the story of the official police dog doesn't really begin until the final years of the last century. In 1888 bloodhounds were brought into the Jack the Ripper case in an attempt to sniff out the murderer and quell public panic. Unfortunately in test sessions there was some confusion and the dogs' value was underrated. It took many years before they were looked to again as a valuable source of police assistance.

On the Continent, however, the attitude was quite different. By World War I dogs had been trained as guards, sentries and messengers and the Alsatian had established its suitability in such roles. In 1934 the Home Office showed an interest and an experimental training school was set up with the result that the first two police dogs, black Labradors, began work in South London in 1938. Then World War II came and plans to train more dogs had to be dropped. In 1946 the training school was re-established, and any question mark that hung over the use of dogs on patrol was dispelled the first night a dog went on duty in Hyde Park. On its first patrol it foiled a purse-snatching attempt and the crime rate in the park plummeted.

Today the Metropolitan Police employ more than 330 dogs. The majority are Alsatians and are used for tracking and searching property and people. Other breeds such as spaniels and retrievers are used for detecting drugs and explosives. Patrol dogs go to live with their handlers at the age of twelve weeks and, if they develop the even temperament and alertness required by police dogs, go on to basic training at the age of twelve months. At the training school in Keston, Kent, they learn how to track and search and 'speak' when they find what they've been looking for. They also learn criminal work and are taught how to disarm attackers with guns, knives and other weapons, and how to control crowds and prisoners. After fourteen weeks of training they are ready to go on the beat with their handlers and cope with situations as diverse as controlling a violent football crowd or, as really happened, finding a couple's engagement ring!

POLICE DOG RATIONS AND EQUIPMENT

These are the rations and equipment officially allocated to Metropolitan Police dogs.

Daily rations:
24 oz meat
16 oz biscuits
8 oz vegetables

Training equipment:
Check chain
Leather collar
Tracking harness
Tracking line

Kennel equipment:
Feeding bowl
Water bowl
Stiff grooming brush
Soft finishing brush
Metal comb
Clinical thermometer
Dumbell
Chamois leather
Brushes
Shovels

FIVE BRAVE POLICE DOGS

Elite was travelling in the car with his handler, PC Keith Hyam, in June 1984 when they sighted a deranged man holding a woman and her two children hostage with a knife. When the woman broke free Elite intervened to prevent the man recapturing her and then gave chase. Unfortunately the man was able to stab him in the head several times and then set about PC Hyam, who was pushed to the ground. Elite managed to come to the aid of his handler and was stabbed again. Bleeding badly, he launched himself for a third time and, despite being stabbed yet again, was able to overpower his attacker and hold him until help came. After treatment from a vet he made a good recovery and went back on police duty.

Kahn In August 1984 PC Alan Bratchell and his Alsatian Kahn were called to an incident at South Croydon Bus Garage where two men were causing criminal damage. They ran away when they saw Kahn coming and he and PC Bratchell chased them. As he rounded a corner PC Bratchell heard a squeal of brakes and found that Kahn had been run over by a car. In desperation he managed to lift the car and free his trapped dog, and Kahn continued the chase and detained the two men before keeling over. A vet later discovered that he had suffered a collapsed lung and internal bleeding, but he soon recovered and returned to duty.

Queenie was killed when a bomb exploded outside Harrods at Christmas in 1983. She was posthumously awarded the RSPCA's highest gallantry award.

Rex III During the 1950s Rex III was one of the first dogs to establish a heroic reputation. He was involved in more than 130 arrests during his career, including one during which he was shot several times.

Yerba In August 1984 Yerba, an Alsatian, was on duty with his handler PC Martin Coxon when they encountered armed men in the act of robbing a security van. One of the robbers had taken a hostage and was holding a gun to his body when Yerba made his attack. Just as he was about to leap the man turned and fired into the dog's chest. Yerba was flung back into the road but made one more effort to launch himself at the robbers before being shot twice more. He died in the arms of his handler and was later buried at the Dog Training Establishment in Keston.

DOGS AND CUSTOMS

By 1988 there will be 56 sniffer dogs working for HM's Customs and Excise, helping to sniff out drugs, firearms and explosives being smuggled into this country. They've become such an accepted and well-known part of the fight against drug smuggling that it's surprising to realise that dogs were only introduced in 1976, after the Customs and Excise department had seen the work being done by the RAF.

The dogs found at ports and airports today are all owned, trained and then loaned out by the RAF. The drug-sniffing dogs, who practise with the real thing but are never allowed to come into direct contact with drugs, can now detect four different types:

Heroin
Cannabis
Cocaine
Amphetamines

The dogs employed to search for firearms and explosives are taught to track twenty different scents, including cordite, gun oil and plastic explosives. All animals are trained to search baggage, freight, aircraft, ships and cars. The most difficult test for them, and one which they all have to pass before they can finish their training, involves searching a ship's engine room where the hot, noisy conditions, slippery floors and conflicting scents of oil and diesel fumes make their task almost impossibly difficult.

Most of the Customs dogs are gun dog breeds – spaniels, Labradors and retrievers. Some are supplied by dogs' homes and others are donated by members of the public who find that the cuddly Weimaraner or springer spaniel they bought as a puppy is too much to handle as it grows up. Only about three per cent of dogs are found to be suitable to undergo training.

Among graduates of the RAF training school is Oscar, who became famous when he demonstrated his sniffing skills for the Princess of Wales during her visit to Heathrow Airport in 1986. While doing another demonstration for the authorities in Guernsey he made unexpected finds of cannabis on board a yacht and two more drugs smugglers were arrested.

Another detector dog, Pip, discovered four tonnes of cannabis hidden in bales of wood at Liverpool Docks in 1986. Also hot on the scent was Ben, a Labrador who sniffed out 82 kilograms of cannabis on board a ship at Montrose docks and a nameless spaniel who, while still in training, detected 2.5 kilograms of cocaine in the ladies' loo at Gatwick Airport. Obviously a star in the making!

But possibly the greatest drug-sniffing dog of them all i Trep, an American golden retriever trained by his police officer owner, Tom Kazo. Within two months of learning his skill he had discovered a haul of hashish on board a shij and in 1979 he was on record as having been responsible for hundred arrests involving drugs worth $63 million.

Perhaps the least successful drug-detection dogs were pair called Laddie and Boy, who were employed during raid in the Midlands in 1967. While their handler questione the two suspects who had been caught as a result of the raid they stroked and petted the clever dogs. After a while Laddi and Boy settled for a snooze in front of the fire, but when the police officer went to arrest the suspects one dog growle menacingly at him and the other jumped up and bit him in the leg . . .

EIGHT GIFTS FROM HARROD. FOR THE PAMPERED POOCH

The Pet Shop at Harrods, the famous Knightsbridge department store, stocks some of the most exclusive and stunning accessories available for dogs. Here's a selection!

1. **A kennel** As you might imagine, Harrods can offer kennel like no other. Try a wooden number with thatched roof. To order, at about £800.
2. If your pet is particularly fond of a snooze, spoil it with wicker **sofa-style bed** upholstered with pillows and cushions. In sizes to suit every dog from about £160.

3. For the pet who likes to create a sensation wherever it goes, a sequined **dog coat** in rainbow colours, complete with tiny top hat and sparkling bow tie. From about £60.

4. Even the most humble mongrel will feel like a million dollars with a gold and *diamanté* **collar** and gold and silver chain **lead**. Prices from around £40.

5. For wet days when you want to keep your dog warm and dry, try a two-piece waterproof nylon **trouser suit**. Prices from £27.

6. No self-respecting dog likes to be dried on a tatty old towel that the family have thrown out. Treat your pet to a Harrods **dog towel**, in discreet green and gold and with the Harrods motif. £5.50 and £8.50, according to size.

7. Turn your dog's dinnertime into a special occasion with a beautiful **dog-shaped china dish**. It's one of the Pet Shop's best-sellers at around £6.

8. Does your dog look lean and fit? Does it love running round the park? If so, give it the professional look with a **jogging suit** in grey, pink or green sweatshirt fabric with hood and ribbing. From around £20.

If these ideas don't appeal, how about a special **four-poster bed** complete with canopy from Brights of Nettlebed, Exeter, at prices up to £1,200 or, from the USA (where else?) a **Dogbrella**? The Dogbrella hooks on to the dog's collar and when the owner pulls the lead in a certain direction a natty little umbrella pops up over the animal's head. Ideal for poodles and other breeds who don't want to ruin their hairdo.

FAVOURITE NAMES FOR DOGS

> Dog, dog – I like a good dog –
> Towser or Bowser or Star –
> Clean sort of pleasure –
> A four-footed treasure –
> And faithful as few humans are.
> > (Scott Fitzerald and Edmund Wilson)

Your dog may not be called Towser or Bowser or Star, but is he called Ben? If so, and you've wondered why every time you call him in the park a dozen strange dogs come running, it's because Ben is the most popular name among British dog-lovers. The petfood manufacturers Spillers commissioned polls of 1,000 owners in 1982 and 1986, and each time Ben came out on top. Of course, all those Bens might have other names in the show ring – but you only have to try yelling 'Witchdale Nathaniel Gnat of Metadale' or 'Vanitonia Wing and a Prayer for Perillan' to see how useful a shorter, if more common, name can be!

1982	1986
1 Ben	Ben
2 Sandy	Cindy
3 Cindy	Sam
4 Kim	Sheba
5 Lassie	Max
6 Sam	Susie
7 Sheba	Penny
8 Prince	Benjy
9 Bonnie	Toby
10 Patch	Sally

Twenty-five years ago most dogs had more traditional names, as this 1962 top ten shows.

1 Rover	6 Duke
2 Prince	7 Rex
3 Lassie	8 Brandy
4 Bob	9 Shep
5 Spot	10 Lucky

TEN SMART NAMES FOR DOGS

In *The Sloane Rover's Handbook*, Francesca Findlater suggests some smart names for equally smart dogs. Here are ten of the best.

1 Phideaux (it's all in the spelling!)
2 Tatler (or Vogue or Harpers, whichever is your favourite)
3 Harrods (or Fortnums or Simpsons)

4 Diana (or any other royal name)
5 Truffle (or caviare or champagne)
6 Alphonse (after the Duchess of Argyll's dog)
7 Spott (notice the spelling)
8 Henry for a dog, Caroline for a bitch
9 Paris (London, New York, China and Rome are equally smart, but Yugoslavia and Czechoslovakia are not so catchy)
10 Battersea (also Chelsea, Mayfair, Knightsbridge and Belgravia but not Ealing, Tottenham or Peckham)

DOG ENDS

'The misery of keeping a dog is his dying so soon. But to be sure if he lived fifty years, and then died, what would become of me?' asked Sir Walter Scott when his beloved mongrel Camp left for those doggy Elysian fields where there's always a cat to chase, a fire to lie by and a bone to chew. The desolation that many dog-owners experience when their pet dies is just as profound as that experienced at the loss of a human friend – perhaps more so, because no human could rival a dog for unquestioning love and loyalty. That's why epitaphs to dogs are so touching. Here are just a few.

> READER
> If you would be beloved and regretted
> Profit by the example of
> DASH
> (Epitaph to Queen Victoria's favourite dog)

Although beneath this grave-mound thy white bones now
are lying
surely, my huntress Lycas, the wild things dread thee still.
(Attributed to Simonides, 556–468 BC)

Be comforted, little dog, and know that at the Resurrection
you too shall have a golden tail.

Though once a puppy, and though Fop by name,
Here moulders one, whose bones some honour claim;
No sycophant, although of Spaniel race!
And though no hound, a martyr to the chase!
Ye squirrels, rabbits, leverets, rejoice!
Your haunts no longer echo to his voice
This record of his fate exulting view –
He died worn out with vain pursuit of you.
'Yes!' the indignant shade of Fop replies,
'And worn with vain pursuit, man also dies.'
('Epitaph on Fop', by William Cowper)

He who out-bounded time and space,
The fleetest of the greyhound race,
Lies here! At length subdued by death,
His speed now stopped and out of breath.
(Epitaph to Snowball, a prize-winning eighteenth-century
greyhound)

Charity, dog of Gideon Bligh,
Underneath this stone doth lie,
Nought was she e'er known to do
That her master told her to.

TIPPY
Sit, boy, and stay
Until I come to join you.
          (From East Sussex)

Writing after the death of Kaiser, his dachshund, Matthew
Arnold summed up perfectly the way a dog continues to be a
presence even after death:

We stroke thy broad, brown paws again,
We bid thee to thy vacant chair,
We greet thee by the window-pane,
We hear thy scuffle on the stair.
                    ('Kaiser Dead', Matthew Arnold)

Perhaps the most famous of all epitaphs to dogs was
written by Lord Byron, whose Newfoundland Boatswain
had a fit and died in front of him in 1808. The poet built a
tomb for him at his home, Newstead Abbey, intending to be
buried alongside him. Unfortunately things didn't go to plan
and the house, and tomb, had to be sold. This is Boatswain's
epitaph:

Oh you who, by chance, see this simple urn, pass on! It
honours no one you would weep for. These stones have
been raised on the remains of a friend. I have known only
one, and he lies here!